STYLE

STYLE

by Elsa Klensch
with Beryl Meyer

Illustrations by David Croland
Photographs by Randy Brooke

A Perigee Book

A Perigee Book
Published by The Berkley Publishing Group
200 Madison Avenue
New York, NY 10016
Copyright © 1995 by Elsa Klensch.
Interior photographs copyright © 1995 by Randy Brooke.

Book design by H. Roberts Design.

Cover design by Joseph Perez.
Cover photo by Douglas Dubler.

First edition: September 1995

Published simultaneously in Canada.

LIBRARY OF CONGRESS CATALOGING-IN-PUBLICATION DATA
Klensch, Elsa
    Style / Elsa Klensch with Beryl Meyer. — 1st ed.
        p.   cm.
    "A Perigee book. "
    ISBN: 0-399-52152-6 (pbk. : acid-free paper)
    1. Clothing and dress—Handbooks, manuals, etc. 2. Beauty,
Personal—Handbooks, manuals, etc. 3. Fashion—Handbooks, manuals,
etc. I. Meyer, Beryl.   II. Title.
TT507 . K617 1995
646' .34—dc20   95-11439

Printed in the United States of America

10 9 8 7 6 5 4 3 2 1

This book is printed on acid-free paper.

Acknowledgments

To the designers, stylists, models, and hair and makeup artists I worked with over the years. Their sensitivity, generosity and vision have made this book possible.

A special thank-you to those whose photographs appear in the book.

Lastly, to my good friends Patricia, Chuck and Jerry.

Contents

Foreword

Style is a powerful thing. Style commands attention and respect, even when a woman is not beautiful. A stylish woman can go anywhere and achieve anything. A stylish woman gets the best table in a restaurant, has the taxi stop for her on a rainy day, and receives better service in department stores and from her own hairdresser.

During nearly twenty-five years in the fashion world, I've seen beautiful women come and go while the stylish ones stay on, building their careers.

Style is not about beauty, wealth, or even fashion. Style is rooted in a woman's knowing herself well enough to develop a consistent image, and then having the courage to project that image.

1

How This Style Expert Developed Her Own Style

*L*ong before I joined CNN and long before my work at *Vogue* and *Harper's Bazaar*, I was aware of the importance of style, and the pleasure to be had developing it. I must have been five or six when my mother bought me the first piece of clothing I vividly remember—a simple smock with a matching belt. Standing in front of the mirror, I tried it first with the sash on and then with it off, deciding which suited me better. I was first becoming aware of my style and the different looks I could create for myself.

Today I wouldn't hesitate. The sash would go. Over time, I learned that simple shapes suit me best.

Much as I love clothes, I've always been practical about them. Owning too many confuses me and I find I end up wearing the same wisely chosen outfits over and over again.

So when I left my hometown of Sydney, Australia, to seek my fortune as a journalist in London, my luggage was light. My one big splurge was a black suit by the French designer Jacques Fath that I'd bought on sale at David Jones department store. I can still remember standing in the fitting room looking at myself from all angles and worrying about whether I should buy it.

The suit cost more than I'd planned, but it fit in well with my black, grey, red, and white wardrobe. And it proved to be money very well spent. The cut was unmistakably French, and it gave me great style. I found when I wore it I felt confident and comfortable at cocktail and dinner parties. What's more, when the editor of the paper where I eventually got a job saw me in it, he decided I should go to Paris to cover the couture collections.

My French suit got me my first trip to Paris. It also taught me a lot about the value of well-designed

clothes. They give confidence. They open doors. They can create an illusion of power which can help you get whatever it is you want.

I always wanted a successful career. And I built my style with that in mind. I dress to suit my career, but also to allow my personality to show through and, most importantly, to please myself.

I enjoy well-made clothes in good fabrics, whether they are traditional like wool or cotton or the latest stretch blend like nylon/Lycra or viscose. And I enjoy trying clothes on—something I believe is most important. Trying clothes on is the only way to get the feel of the fabric, to evaluate the ease of the cut, and to see the effect of the color on the skin.

On several occasions, when a designer has suggested I try on a jacket or a coat, I've done so out of politeness—never suspecting I would like it. Then, to my amazement, I discovered it made me look terrific. It's a good lesson to remember. No one's eye, or experience, for that matter, is infallible.

My pursuit of style continued in London. I was starting to recognize what was—and wasn't—"me." In those early years when I was in my twenties, I was never interested in owning a ball gown. What fascinated me were those great day clothes. They were wonderfully fitting and so well-pulled-together with accessories. And the quality was unparalleled.

When it came to evening I chose separates because

they could create many different moods, unlike a ball gown. For evening was the time to be feminine, not grand, rich, or even luxurious.

My writing career soon took me to Hong Kong. While I was there, I met my American journalist husband, married him in wartime Saigon, and then came to live in New York City.

Manhattan terrified me at first, but after landing a job as a fashion editor at *Women's Wear Daily*, I quickly discovered that New York was the fashion capital of America, if not of the world.

Exciting things were happening in New York in the seventies. American designers Calvin Klein, Bill Blass, Anne Klein, and Ralph Lauren were beginning to climb the ladder to international fame. I was there to follow every fashion and every fad.

Of course, my own style changed over the years. Who could resist the fun of that fashion explosion that took place in the seventies? But certain things remained constant: the quality of the clothes I bought and my favorite basic colors.

I also changed jobs during the mid-seventies, working as a fashion editor at *Vogue* and then as senior fashion editor at *Harper's Bazaar*. Then, in 1980, I got the chance to put fashion where I had always thought it belonged—on television.

Having my own show at CNN has been the greatest experience of my career. Interviewing design-

ers, stylists, models, hairdressers, and makeup artists has taught me more about fashion and style than I could ever have learned anywhere else.

It certainly reinforced my belief that style is important to every one of us. And that's what this book is all about. It should help you find the path that works for you. It should show you how to choose clothes that are timeless, and looks that bring out your best features. No matter where you live, no matter what your budget is—you can have great style.

2

How to Cultivate

Your Style

Any woman can have style. The challenge is developing it. Going into the best shops and buying expensive clothes won't necessarily help. It takes a different type of investment—one that requires less money, but a lot of time and effort.

Style comes with understanding your needs and lifestyle and, even more importantly, it comes with respecting and enjoying yourself as a unique person, an individual. By that, I mean learning to accept what you can't change, and focusing, more positively, on your assets.

There's a freedom that comes with saying to yourself: "This is all I can ever be, but I can and will make the most of it."

Be as attractive as you possibly can—the *best you* possible. Package yourself so you can be happy in your skin and content with the impression you make in all the various aspects of your life.

All the stylish women I know make effective use of three key personal preferences to achieve their distinctive looks:

Hairstyle—Well-groomed hair cut in proportion to your figure attracts immediate attention and establishes you as a person who cares about her appearance.

Color—It draws attention to your face, and it can make you appear taller, slimmer, more vibrant, and more confident.

Accessories—More than any other element, they indicate the sort of person you are—quiet and discreet, or strong and forceful. For work, your accessories should always be the best quality you can

afford. You can make a cheap outfit look expensive with quality accessories, but cheap accessories will ruin the most expensive dress.

PITFALLS TO AVOID

The first step in developing style often entails moving out of your mother's shadow (no matter how old you are) and nurturing your spirit.

It takes conviction and work; it's easy to get lost when you try to be too many things to too many people. When you don't concentrate on yourself, style suffers. It becomes erratic, diluted, unfocused.

Don't be surprised if family and friends try to dissuade you when they see you developing style. They'll question your preference for pants, or a particular color. Most likely they're feeling intimidated; someone who has style has identity and power. Because they are insecure, they might try to convince you to dress as they do. *Don't* be swayed by them. What looks great on your best friend can be disastrous on you.

Remember, the worst reason in the world to buy something is because it looks good on a friend or a TV actress. Don't let glamour blind you.

Zero in on the style of the most important person in your life—*you*.

FIRST STEPS

Style starts with being realistic about your body. Genes can't be ignored: If your ancestors had characteristically big chests, as my solidly built Swiss forebears did, the fact is, you'll never have a slender upper body. On the other hand, you may have enviably slim hips.

You have to find a balance. I wear dark tops (to make my bust look smaller) with a bright or a pale bottom (to show off my legs).

Study your proportions—whether you're short, tall, thin, or round—until you know everything about your figure. Then you can begin to understand which proportions work for you.

Just as essential in developing your style is finding the colors that are most flattering to your skin tone. You'll do best when you make the colors that flatter you the basis of your wardrobe—for work and play, for day and night—and stick to them.

I learned most about style while taking part in the editorial "run-throughs" at *Vogue*. At these meetings the fashion editors pull in the best clothes in the market and dissect them in terms of success or failure. From these sessions I developed a sense of proportion and color. I also became adept at analyzing why one particular outfit worked while another didn't.

And these are the skills I'm offering you. I've put this book together to help you take the basics that apply to your particular needs and use them as your springboard to style.

Once you've considered the basics, use your imagination to build upon them and you'll have the foundation for a solid, modern wardrobe, one that will target success in all aspects of your life—now and well into the twenty-first century.

One final thought on style: It takes strength to recognize it, confidence to project it, and discipline to maintain it. The good news: The more stylish you are, the happier and the more successful you'll be.

DETERMINE YOUR FIGURE "CHALLENGES" AND FIND YOUR PROPORTIONS

As many women as there are in the world, and as varied our shapes, we all have certain areas of our bodies that can be a challenge to overcome. These are our own personal hang-ups, or sore spots, and everyone has them. While some women may appear to have the perfect figure, it may be because they know how to dress to play up their assets and downplay what they don't like about their bodies.

You can easily do the same. No matter what

your sensitive area—whether it's that you perceive yourself as being top- or bottom-heavy, high- or low-waisted (or not having a waist), short-legged or heavy-thighed—you can compensate for it by accentuating your positive points.

Quick Tricks to Find Your Proportions

- Squint (rather than staring wide-eyed) at your reflection in the mirror. A tighter gaze will block out those distracting lumps and bumps, and allow a clearer focus as to your overall body shape.

- Give as much time to side and back views as to the front. In order to honestly judge your shape, you have to really see the evidence!

- An easy way to tell if you're short- or long-waisted without measuring is to gauge the distance from your neck to your waist and from waist to crotch. If the upper half is longer, you're long-waisted, and vice-versa.

- Determine the length of your neck and legs (they play an important part in overall proportion) with these simple tests:

  - If you can easily touch your chin to your chest, your neck is short; if you have to strain, it's long.

  - If the distance from shoulders to crotch is longer than from crotch to ankles, you're short-legged.

Mirror Tricks

The easiest way to learn about your own shape is to put on a leotard and pantyhose, stand in front of your full-length mirror, and have a friend outline your figure with a grease pencil. Step back and study the drawing closely, taking note of the distances between neck, bust, waist, hips, and legs.

Take a realistic view of yourself without being too critical. Then list your good points: square shoulders . . . narrow waist . . . smooth stomach . . . long legs. We all have positive attributes that we can feel good about. Knowing these by heart helps you make the right decisions. It's a form of conditioning.

Make a point of looking at it every time you go out; really examine yourself—not just your hair and makeup, but the overall image you project. It pays, believe me.

Sketching

Another way to increase your awareness of your figure is to draw a few sketches of your body. They don't have to be done with precision and skill—just with an honest perception of your body's shape. This is the best way to reinforce your consciousness of your strengths and challenges.

You'll find a mental sketch pops into your head when you're looking at clothes. Gradually, you'll

The best advice I can give you is to regard your mirror as a friend, not an enemy.

recognize those characteristics you're less than happy with almost instantly. Knowing how to compensate for them is one of the best-kept secrets of a stylish woman.

Photographs

A third way to gain self-knowledge about your body is to draw an outline of your figure on a photograph.

Photos can also help you maintain a positive body image. I keep a snapshot of myself all dressed up on my makeup table as a reminder that I *can* look good all the time. It serves as a reference point: When I'm not up to snuff, I can look at that picture and figure out why.

Go through your photo albums and pull those shots you feel are your best, and worst. Chances are you'll be wearing the same type of clothes in all your favorite pictures. Seeing yourself in your clothes and makeup will give you a new perspective: You'll be more in control once you see how they function for you.

Videotape

Do what the TV anchors do: Gauge your looks with videotape.

Ask a friend or relative who has a video camera to shoot some tape of you in different outfits, hairstyles, and makeup. Experiment. You can learn a

great many things by watching the tape and looking at yourself objectively.

Initially it's difficult. The lighting on TV tends to make you look slightly heavier. While a home video will also distort your weight, the advantage of using it is that it enables you to look at details you wouldn't ordinarily see. Concentrate on the proportion of your body, your posture, the colors against your skin . . . and whether you look comfortable in your clothes.

Most of the people I know in television watch themselves continuously. By doing so, they're able to surmount their self-consciousness and analyze their performance dispassionately. And that is the key—being dispassionate.

You'll soon get beyond that initial feeling of "Oh, no! I look awful in that outfit," and start to reason why. Ask yourself why it doesn't work for your body. Being aware of the mistake prevents you from making it again. And don't forget: It's just as important to focus on why something *works* and what you're doing *right*!

Seeing myself on video so much, I learned to dissect my figure and features. I used to drop my head when I was interviewing on-camera so I would look more approachable. But when I saw the tape, I realized that dropping my head made me look unsure of myself. I found what works better is to keep my chin up and to lift my body from my rib cage—that's the best posture-booster I know, as it squares your shoulders and lengthens your neck.

Thanks to video, I also know I look my best, and slimmest, when I'm wearing a tunic or long jacket (to downplay my bust, the top needs to be collarless or simple-collared, and single-breasted) with either straight or slightly tapered pants, or a skirt of the same style (to play up my long legs). It's a uniform I rely on endlessly, and one in which I feel most confident when I add my personal touches.

It took several sessions of watching myself on camera before I became aware of how really long my face is. To shorten it, I started wearing bangs.

I found that one cheekbone is higher than the other, one eye wider, and one brow lower. This isn't something I feel bad about; no one's face is perfectly symmetrical. To achieve a balance, I brush on blush a little lower on the raised cheekbone and apply a touch more makeup to the smaller eye.

It's all a matter of self-acceptance. Work *with* nature—it's so much easier than fighting it. Forget about contouring, or creating a high-fashion profile. Most of those so-perfect fashion magazine photos of supermodels have been retouched on a computer—and who can compete with that?

To achieve the look you want, work around your challenges and accentuate your best features.

As important as clothes and makeup are to your image, so, too, are carriage, posture, and a sense of confidence. Check them out on the video. Do you project self-assuredness or insecurity, vitality or a lack of interest? Once you're aware of your body language and how you express yourself, then you can learn to present yourself better. Carriage, posture and a positive self-image are essential parts of the "package," so chin up!

Should you be unhappy with your look on-camera, an exercise program is an excellent way to get in touch with your body, and to deal with your weight as well as your carriage. This takes discipline but, believe me, you'll not only look better, you'll feel a lot better.

Top-heavy

TOP-HEAVY FIGURE DOs & DON'Ts

DO spend as much time as is necessary finding the
right bra or body suit. It can make a world of difference. Your best buy is a no-seam bra that offers a
natural-looking profile.

DO go for collarless jackets and avoid patch breast
pockets. The less detail on or near your bust,
the less attention you'll attract to it.

DON'T ever forget that a tight sweater is your
worst enemy. The next worst is a light top
worn over a dark bottom.

DON'T wear wide belts. They'll make
your bosom look even bigger.

SMALL-BUSTED FIGURE DOs & DON'Ts

DO experiment with layering. You can wear a vest over a shirt in
winter, or a bandeau bra under one in summer.

DO dare to go braless in the evening. Small breasts under a sweater
look sexier than you can imagine.

DON'T forget that with your small bust you look wonderful in mannish
jackets, and this is a plus if you're climbing the executive ladder.

DON'T forget also that with your figure you can get away with the most
romantic ruffles, wide bertha collars, and peasant shirts.

BOTTOM-HEAVY FIGURE DOs & DON'Ts

DO avoid different skirt lengths. Find the one that is most flattering to your proportions and stay with it.

DO keep pantyhose and shoes in tone with skirts and pants, to elongate your figure.

DON'T choose light colors for skirts and pants—you'll only draw attention to your lower torso. Remember, dark colors make heavy areas look smaller.

DON'T stop experimenting with tops. Use them to draw attention to your well-proportioned bust and to flatter your face.

Bottom-heavy

HIGH-WAISTED FIGURE DOs & DON'Ts

DO wear all one color from neckline to hemline.

DO opt for a sheath dress whenever possible. Its straight shape elongates your waistline—and it's more flattering than any other style.

DON'T tuck your blouse or pullover in as it will broadcast exactly where your waist is. Your best length is exactly three inches below—just where your stomach starts to rise.

DON'T wear contrasting belts. Your smartest choice is a narrow one-inch-wide style that is simply designed and toned to match your pants or skirt.

LOW-WAISTED FIGURE DOs & DON'Ts

DO emphasize your waist with belts. Sashes in contrasting colors are especially flattering.

DO watch the fit of jackets as they are often too short-waisted. A very fitted jacket will be cut too high. Save your money—it'll never feel right on you.

DON'T buy skirts or pants with a wide waistband. Too often, the waist will rise so high, it'll be uncomfortable.

DON'T consider a princess-lined or fitted coat; it will only accentuate your low waist. With that long back, you'll look like a million dollars in a bathrobe coat tied low.

STRAIGHT-UP-AND-DOWN FIGURE DOs & DON'Ts

DO choose skirts, pants and jackets that tie softly at the waist. That gentle gathering creates the illusion of a waistline.

DO—especially if your neck is long—play with long scarves and necklaces. These will give your torso the illusion of shape.

DON'T mix too many colors. A soft, simple print is best for you.

DON'T wear tight belts. Your best bet is the belt that lies easily and loosely on your hips.

Straight-bodied

SHORT-LEGGED FIGURE DOs & DON'Ts

DO match your stockings to your shoes and skirts or pants. That continuous line of color elongates the leg.

DO keep your trouser legs slim and straight to help create the illusion of height.

DON'T wear cuffed trousers. Even a small cuff will cut your height.

DON'T wear skirts below the knee. They'll only chop you in half.

HEAVY-THIGHED FIGURE DOs & DON'Ts

DO choose loose-fitting pants and skirts, such as a flared A-line style. (Avoid anything bias-cut as it will cling.) Wear fitted tops with them to show off the smallness of your body.

DO collect tunic-length tops or even large tees to give you the coverage you need.

DON'T wear prints, horizontal stripes, or bright colors below the waist. These will only draw attention to thighs.

DON'T forget a body shaper if you must wear a more fitted look. A long-leg controller trims hips and thighs for a smoother, sleeker line.

COLOR: ONE OF YOUR MOST POWERFUL TOOLS

Because of my skin tone, I've worn black or brown with white, ivory, or red as long as I can remember. When you're born looking 29 years old, as I was—with a long face that makes it virtually impossible to appear cute and girlish—black is the naturally sophisticated color choice.

I strayed once. TV veterans warned me that black should never be worn on television because of the lighting, so I went for dusty pastels. Big mistake. They made me look totally washed out, and I felt perpetually tired in such faded colors. The lesson cost me a great deal of money: I gave away some very expensive pastel clothing.

Because colors play such an important part in our lives, you must find the ones that work best for you. They're the ones you must wear and learn to use effectively as you develop your personal style.

Color commands attention and respect. It refreshes your eye and cheers you up enormously when you're tired. And better than anything else, it draws attention to your face.

I'm all for color in the office, too. I don't mean dizzying, distracting brights, but "up" colors such as the great jewel tones of emerald, ruby, and sapphire.

A woman loses authority when she wears pastels in the office. Pretty pales—even beiges and greys—

tend to be too soft and feminine. And forget light blues and pinks—except as secondary pieces, sweaters or blouses.

How to Find Your Best Colors

One of the big developments in the cosmetics industry in the late eighties was color coding for different skin shades. This started as a way to sell cosmetics but has become an increasingly valuable service to help customers find the fashion colors that are right for them.

Experts say that most complexions fall into two color categories: yellow-orange or blue-red. When you determine your skin shade you should wear both makeup and fashions in the same color range.

Many makeup companies have refined the color coding even further and offer as many as four different choices. Princess Marcella Borghese and Origins are among the growing number of companies that offer this service. You can ask representatives at either makeup counter to help determine your personal color code.

Prescriptives offers these four choices:

Yellow-orange—skin with golden undertones
Red-orange—skin with peach undertones
Red—skin with pale pink undertones
Blue-red—skin with blue/pink undertones.

Prescriptives maintains that when a woman uses makeup in the colors that suit her skin she will always look her best. If you take that principle one step further and keep your clothes toned to your particular colors, your style will be strong, lasting, and immensely flattering.

The following color-coding charts offer guidelines for making clothing choices that will mesh well with your skin tone. Fashion colors are the colors you should use for big pieces of clothing—jackets, blouses, or sweaters—that are worn near your face. Accent colors can be part of a pattern, a scarf or pocket square, or a T-shirt or camisole worn under a fashion color.

Y E L L O W - O R A N G E

Suggested fashion colors
Deep brown
Bitter chocolate
✓Camel
Gold
✓Mustard
✓Terracotta
✓Rust
Rust with a touch of orange

Avoid
True red

Suggested accent colors
Pumpkin
Teal blue
✓Lime green
Jade green
Olive green

. . . .

R E D - O R A N G E

Suggested fashion colors
Warm brown
Golden brown
Beige
✓Camel
Light navy

Avoid
Pink

Suggested accent colors
Salmon
Coral
Apricot
Bright yellow-green
Clear aqua
✓Turquoise
✓Ivory
Golden brown

. . . .

R E D

Suggested fashion colors	*Suggested accent colors*
Navy	Lavender
Charcoal	Mauve
Deep grey	Rose
Blue grey	Fuchsia
Burgundy	Plum
Brown with a touch of red	Rose pink
Rose brown	Blue-red
	Sky blue
Avoid	Green with a touch
Yellow	of blue

B L U E - R E D

Suggested fashion colors	*Suggested accent colors*
Any true color	Icy pink
Black	Icy violet
Pure white	Icy green
Charcoal grey	Hot turquoise
Grey taupe	Deep pink
Taupe	Bright fuchsia
Navy blue	Burgundy
	Blue-red
Avoid	True red
Orange	

"

Remind yourself how great you can look!

Tape the best photos of
yourself inside your
wardrobe door or at the side
of your makeup mirror. Use
the pictures as a guide, a reference point, when getting
ready in the morning, so you
begin to train and discipline yourself to
wear only what is flattering to you.

I believe in the color-coding system as a good way to start finding what suits you. Of course, when you gain confidence you can play around with colors—but not until you really feel good about judging what flatters your skin tone.

Go to two or three cosmetic companies for advice before making any decisions. Don't be intimidated by the sales staff. There's no reason to buy even a lipstick until you've checked out their system.

If you're really in doubt, splurge on an independent makeup artist—one who is *not* employed by a cosmetics company. Check with your hair salon. They often do photography shoots, such as weddings, and some of them even have an on-premise makeup artist. He or she should give you unbiased advice. But go prepared, with a full list of problems and questions you'd like to solve.

Which Colors Come First

Neutrals—black, brown, grey, navy, taupe, beige—must be the basis of your working wardrobe.

Pick the ones that suit you and you feel comfortable in. Also take into account the climate and other aspects of your life.

The best way to find the right colors for your basic wardrobe is to hold things up to your face in front of a mirror. But watch the light. Fluorescent lights in a fitting room can distort the impact color

NEUTRALS: THE WAY TO START

The colors you choose to anchor your wardrobe require the staying power offered by the three color families of the classic neutrals:

Grey/black (cool tones)—These shades range from charcoal grey to silver and all the intensities of black.

Navy/taupe/grey (either cool or warm tones)—Navy is a bewitching color. It's well worth considering if you're over 40 because it's kinder to the face than black. It looks great with soft beiges and it's striking with greys.

Brown/beige (warm tones)—A range of warm colors from the palest cream through tan, to dark chocolate.

The best plan is to buy pieces such as jackets, pants, and skirts in solid neutrals. Then collect blouses, sweaters, and accessories in rich or lively accent colors. The advantage to building a wardrobe based upon these basics is that you can use them all across the board: They're businesslike, powerful, luxurious.

Each neutral color family benefits from a fresh, bright touch of white (best for those with blue skin tones) or ivory (most compatible with yellow undertones). A shirt, blouse, sweater, or cardigan in either color reflects light and draws attention to the face.

has upon your skin. Daylight will give you your truest reading. Look for a mirror that's near a window or a source of natural lighting.

Consider your makeup as well. If you're not wearing your usual shade of foundation, your judgment will be off. And if you're sans makeup, colors that normally would suit you may make you look washed-out.

What's on or near your face can affect how successful or not a color is for you. If black doesn't suit you, but you want to include it in your wardrobe, a black shirt with a white or ivory collar can be just the solution. That touch of lightness gives most complexions a flattering lift. And because the collar literally frames your face, it makes black infinitely more wearable.

I don't think, however, you should buy a dress in a color you can't wear and then put on a scarf. If you have to rely on accessories to make a dress or a one-piece look better suited to your skin tone, you'll quickly find it's boring and it's too much trouble.

3

Building a Career Wardrobe That Works

(As Hard As You Do)

Since you spend so much time at work, a large part of your wardrobe are your career separates. But there's no reason you shouldn't love what you wear to the office. And there's no reason your career basics shouldn't take you into evening, and even into the weekend. So building a solid versatile work wardrobe is very important.

Looking good at work is vital to your career.

What you wear in the office tells others what you think about yourself and your job—even what you expect from life.

The more polished and professional you appear, the sooner you'll be promoted, and the sooner you'll have more money and authority. That's what power dressing is all about.

People at the top dress in a confident, realistic way. They choose easy, unaffected clothes that combine classic proportions with quality fabrics in neutral shades. And they make use of pattern effectively, lending dash and drama to their look.

I'm often asked, "How much should I spend on clothes?" The answer is simple: "as much as you can afford to spend." Work clothing should be viewed as an investment.

When a job applicant walks into my office, I automatically size up what the person is wearing: the quality, cut, and how it's all put together. I'm not interested in the *price*. I'm interested in *style*. From that first glance I can get a good idea if a woman really cares about building a successful career, based on how much she cares about her appearance. Your clothes will be similarly judged by the men and women you meet in your job. And dressing well will help you reach your goal.

When you dress for work, project your intelli-

gence first and your femininity second. That is, keep the focus on your face, not on your great legs, perfectly manicured hands, or narrow waist. Jewelry should highlight the face, a blouse or scarf should bring color to it, and well-cut, clean hair should frame it.

If you're speaking at or chairing a meeting, or making a presentation, heighten the focus on your face. Wear a bright color, add a gold necklace or a beautiful scarf—that touch of glamour will help you hold the audience. When a woman exhibits a certain flair and creativity in her clothes, she appears to have something to offer—she creates interest and gains a higher regard. And the audience will sit up and take notice.

But for the day-to-day routine, stay with the basic looks, your colors, and your well-proportioned clothes. You build credibility when you dress consistently. Remember, no one judges you as harshly as your workmates—the people who want your job, or fear you may get theirs.

When choosing your career clothes, keep in mind what's appropriate to your profession and your own work setting. Is it formal or informal, corporate or creative? The workplace, in general, is getting more casual. But your selections will greatly depend upon the tone of your office. Look at the most successful women in the company to see how they dress, then follow suit.

To be a success, you must look like a success, no matter how young you are or how far up the executive ladder you have to go.

Experiment with different workday looks at night or during the weekend. That's when you have everything to gain and nothing to lose. If a look works—if you feel good about yourself in something—incorporate it into your career wardrobe. Programming your wardrobe for work means zeroing in on the simplest formula—selecting a skeleton number of comfortable separates that can be easily coordinated for an enormous variety of neat, professional looks. Don't be lazy about it. Putting together a lean, high-quality wardrobe will save you expense and time. You won't waste money on clothing that will wear out or go out of style—or worse, clothes that will hang in your closet unworn. And ultimately, your new style, your flair, and confidence will pay off in the form of career advancement.

GAIN POWER, AUTHORITY, AND CONFIDENCE THROUGH:

- Strong or stylish accessories that are classic and sophisticated.
- Jewelry that's kept close to the face.
- Heels, medium to high, that will bring you to eye level with most men.
- Expertly applied, natural-looking makeup.
- A smart, well-maintained hairstyle.

Important Tips for Power Dressing

- Find a comfortable weight level and stay within a couple of pounds of it. It's the secret to having a nonstop wardrobe.

- Dress appropriately for your place of work. You must fit into your surroundings. If you work for a large corporation, you'll need a different wardrobe than you would for a small advertising firm.

- Your clothes have to be easy to maintain, so they don't eat into your time or take up too much of your budget with dry cleaning.

- Learn about modern fabrics—more and more blends have the look of natural fibers but the easy care of synthetics. Even designers who make expensive clothes for executive women are using these great fabrics.

- Remember, fashion should add enjoyment—not stress—to your life. You have to get dressed every day, but it shouldn't be a routine duty like brushing your teeth; it should be creative and pleasurable.

FIVE TOPS I CAN'T LIVE WITHOUT

Red knit cardigan jacket, slightly fitted. It's single-breasted, has shaped shoulders, and can be worn with a straight skirt or pants. (I wear it with a skirt for business; with silk pajama pants for evening.) It's comfortable, and the shiny gold buttons give me a lift when I put it on.

Black silk sweater tunic with narrow but well-shaped, square shoulders. It goes with matching silk pants and every skirt I own. The shine of the silk makes it glamorous so it's a natural for day-into-evening.

Black-and-white dotted silky blouse. I wear it under a business suit or to the beach with white pants. I like dots. They don't attract too much attention, and they have a vitality that's always fresh.

Dusty pink tunic sweater with a high turtleneck. I wear it in the office when I'm tired of jackets and want something more comfortable. It looks good with a snappy straight skirt, bold earrings, and lots of bracelets. I get the most wear from it on the weekend.

Black-and-white houndstooth jacket. It's a bit sporty for *serious* business wear, but I dress it up with smart pins, and always team it with a skirt. A natural for traveling—for work and pleasure—it looks as good with jeans as with leggings.

DOs & DON'Ts FOR SHOPPING SMART

DO try everything on and consider each garment carefully, going over in your mind the good and bad points of each. It's really the only way to know if something suits you.

DO go back to a shop where you've found a designer label that fits both your body and your price range. Designers tend to work with the same figure type in mind, and if you're happy with a jacket, chances are you'll like other pieces as well.

DO keep up with what's happening in the fashion industry. The more aware you are, the easier it is to make current looks work for you.

DO, when shopping for a particular item, take along what you plan to wear with it, to make sure color and style are compatible. If you're buying a jacket, for instance, bring along a skirt and pants to check the proportions.

DO try to limit yourself to buying only replacement pieces, once you've built your wardrobe. Think long and hard before pulling out your wallet.

DON'T buy anything unless you have *three* pieces you can wear it with. Of course there *are* exceptions—when you find something that works wonders for you. It could be a little black dress if you have a great figure, fabulous drop earrings if you have a long neck, or sensationally sexy shoes if you have shapely legs.

DON'T go shopping unless you're in the mood for it, prepared, and know exactly how much money you have to spend. If, like me, you're one of those women who sometimes shops to reward herself, then make a list of the things you really need and carry it with you. It helps stop impulse buying.

DON'T rush, no matter how harried you feel. You may have to live with the decision for seasons.

DON'T be influenced by others, especially sales clerks, who may be thinking more about their commissions than about your best interests.

DON'T settle. If it doesn't feel good, it doesn't look good.

DOs & DON'Ts FOR CLOTHING CARE

DO remove large, bulky labels from clothes. They bunch up at the neck and detract from a clean line. Worse, they may show through the fabric.

DO become an expert at hand-washing and ironing. It's a chore but it reaps rewards in looking good and saving money.

DO invest in a closet organizer. Keep skirts, pants, and blouses separated.

DO buy thin, slip-proof hangers. They take up less room in your closet, and keep things neater.

DO go over your clothes to see if they need repairing before you put them away for the season. Then they'll be ready to wear the minute the weather changes.

DO make sure buttons are substantial and securely fastened; if not, you'll waste time and money replacing them. (Don't forget to check buttons before buying a top. It can be a costly nuisance if you lose one and have to replace a dozen.)

DO cover important pieces, especially ones with expensive detail, with a plastic dry-cleaner bag or a garment bag. Preventing dust collection and discoloring will give your clothes a longer life.

DON'T drop clothes on the floor or throw them over the sofa. Discipline yourself to hang them up the minute you take them off. Then there's no need to iron the next time you want to wear them.

DON'T neglect your shoes. Clean them regularly. Scuff marks and scruffy heels look sloppy.

DOs & DON'Ts FOR FABRICS

DO buy clothes in seasonless fabrics—such as knits, wools (challis, crepe, or gabardine) or wool blends—for the office. Look for ones with a certain crispness and body. They're even more comfortable with a bit of stretch. But fabrics should be lightweight enough so you keep cool at work, no matter how hot it is.

DO buy the best fabrics you can afford. They look rich and last longer. Remember, fabrics are the foundation of fashion.

DO read the fiber information on the label—always, always, always! Ignoring the proper method of care can cost you plenty.

DON'T wear a fabric to work that's too sporty or dressy, such as denim or satin.

DON'T buy fabrics that wrinkle easily. Twist a corner of the garment to see how it stands up.

DON'T close your eyes to the latest innovations in fibers. They're the cornerstone of tomorrow's wardrobe.

COUNT ON QUALITY FABRICS

The best career clothes are rendered in fabrics that look like they've already arrived at the top of the ladder: soft, drape-able . . . in a word, luxurious. It's better to be on the soft side rather than the crisp side when your choosing fabrics. Those with some suppleness to them don't crease as easily. They also look cooler and more sophisticated.

For the most versatility, choose fabrics that easily span the seasons. Today's synthetics have just as long a life as natural fibers—and are as comfortable year-round. Fabric manufacturers are constantly experimenting with man-made fibers, giving them a wide variety of textures, finishes, new durability, and new crease-resistant properties. It is absolutely essential that you read the fabric label on your

Drape is all-important

garment, so that you know what fibers are in it, and how best to care for it. While you have more options now, always buy the best you can afford. The plainest dress can look as if it cost a fortune if the fabric is beautiful.

For a polished look in the office, mix fabrics that have basically the same visual weight. That doesn't mean limiting yourself to just knits or crepes. A wool jacket works beautifully over a twill skirt. On the other hand, a suede jacket is too heavy for a silk skirt. The right mix can energize an outfit. If you don't feel comfortable in it, that's your best clue the combination is off-kilter.

Fiber technology continues and it's on a woman's side. Fabrics are easier than ever to care for. And that's where effortless dressing starts.

PICKING PATTERNS FOR THE OFFICE

Classic is the key word for those prints worn from nine to five. Don't be put off by this; there are dozens of classic prints to choose from. Just look at all the great patterns men have been wearing for years: Glen plaids, houndstooth checks, paisleys, pinstripes, polka dots, and tweeds are just a few. These are all smart choices for work—and for your wardrobe—because they never go out of style.

SEASONLESS FABRICS

All jersey blends
Light wool jersey
Light wool gabardine
Wool or rayon challis
Leather
Suede
Cotton/Lycra blends
        (new ones are woven)
Lightweight double knits in
        cotton, wool, or blends
Silky synthetic knits
All crepes (particularly rayon),
        including crepe de chine
Acrylics
Microfibers
Spandex
Viscose
Polyesters

A blouse or scarf in a subtle print can cheer you and your outfit on a dreary day. A bold pattern, such as an animal or abstract print, is a timeless way to bring a traditional style to life. Floral and whimsical motifs are more for fun, so save them for the weekend.

You can mix patterns in the office for even greater impact. Checks with plaids, a combination of wide and thin stripes—these have the power to stand out and look sophisticated at the same time. For the most successful mix, limit patterns and colors to two or three, and keep them similar in tone. To prevent a dizzying effect, balance the scales of the patterns. Contrast a large print with a smaller one in the same color scheme. That subtle type of difference is interesting and easy on the eye.

Wear the boldest print on those areas you want to highlight. Smaller prints belong only on areas you want to downplay. It's a rule I always follow and you should too, as your figure will always look in proportion.

Straight

Jackets

A jacket is the pivotal element of any wardrobe. It adds sophistication and polish to any piece that anchors it—from skirts to pants to city shorts. And a well-cut jacket can conceal most figure challenges.

A jacket lends presence and importance. It affords women the same authority and power that a man's suit provides. It's the first thing people notice when you're sitting at your desk. And with heating and air-conditioning making work environments seasonless, the jacket has earned its place as a year-round wardrobe item.

Jackets are cut in three basic shapes: straight, fitted, and cardigan-style.

A straight-line jacket should never be really straight. It needs the gentlest curve to be flattering.

A fitted jacket can be as simple as an easy blazer or it can be trendy and snappily cut.

Considerably more relaxed than the others, a cardigan-style jacket, like those of the incomparable Coco Chanel, needs only a minimum of detail to be savvy enough for the office.

Fitted

Cardigan

FINDING THE RIGHT JACKET

• Shoulder fit is all-important. Seams should sit straight and smooth across the shoulders, and the jacket should fall straight.

• If you're tall and thin, shoulders should be broad. Try dolman sleeves. If you're small and narrow, you'll want narrow shoulders and set-in sleeves.

• Well-placed pockets are essential. They can soften the line of a jacket or lend a casual ease, as well as being functional.

• Length is critical: Too short looks skimpy with pants; too long looks dowdy or heavy with a skirt.

• Look for a full lining. It means better quality and it adds to the shape and comfort of the jacket.

• Check for other signs of superior workmanship: neatly finished collar, hem, buttonholes, cuffs, pockets.

• A trendy jacket is a luxury item that you should buy only after you have the basics.

The Style to Choose If . . .

You Want to Minimize a Large Bust

- Opt for single-breasted styles.
- Small-to-medium collars are okay; breast pockets are not.
- Make sure the jacket can be worn comfortably both closed and open. If it pulls even slightly at the bust, it's not for you.
- Keep details to a minimum.
- Avoid exaggerated shapes such as dolman sleeves, which tack on extra inches, or waist-cinching styles that emphasize what's on top.
- Go for dark color, a thin vertical stripe pattern, to downplay size.
- Your best fabrics are flat—jerseys or crepes. Those with some dimension, like mohair or wool bouclé, visually increase size.

The Style to Choose If . . .

You Want to Shrink a Large Bottom

- Select jackets that fall past the derriere. Fingertip length is a good guideline.
- Choose from a variety of loosely fitted or flared styles, such as the straight or A-line jacket, to camouflage heaviness.

IF YOU CAN ONLY AFFORD ONE GREAT WARDROBE BASIC, MAKE IT . . .

A jacket. Ultimately, it moves around your wardrobe in many different ways—with pants, skirts, bike shorts, a bathing suit, and so much more.

• Opt for a jacket with well-shaped shoulders to balance your torso. Details that bring the eye up—such as epaulets—can really help.

• Slash or diagonal pockets can trim inches off your hips. Leave them sewn up for a smoother, flatter line. Avoid patch or cuffed pockets.

• Avoid fully- or half-belted waists if your waistline is small and completely out of proportion to your hips. It will only bring more attention to them.

THE STYLE TO CHOOSE IF . . .

You Want to Make Your Neck Look Longer

• Choose collarless or V-necked styles that elongate.
• Under them wear V-necked or low crew sweaters (making certain the neckline comes *under* the jacket collar line).
• Also try shirts that you can enliven with a string of beads.
• Collect wrap blouses that follow the line of a V-necked jacket.

SKIRTS

A slim skirt—whether straight, A-line, pleated, or wrapped—is best for work. It's the most businesslike cut, and the most useful as a quick and able partner for a jacket, sweater, or blouse. Worn inventively, the same skirt can take you straight through the work week.

The simpler the skirt the better, and the longer it will be in style. The requirements for longevity are few. Ideally, it should have a narrow waistband with loops. Elastic in the back helps to ensure a good fit. The hem should be about two inches wide (so the skirt falls properly) and meticulously finished.

THE THREE PERFECT HEMLINES

Each woman has three hemlines that are perfect for her legs: above the knee, below the knee, and below the calf.

To find your perfect skirt lengths, stand in front of a full-length mirror and note the three places where your leg naturally curves in.

On most women, one spot is about four inches above the knee; another is about one inch below the knee; and the third falls about two inches below the

Wrap skirt

Clothes designed by Calvin Klein

widest part of the calf. Because of the indentations in your leg, a hemline that skims any of these three points gives the illusion of slimness above it.

Of course, short skirts look younger and are more comfortable on a busy schedule. But if you're not proud of your knees or thighs, and don't like dark-toned hose (a great disguise for less-than-perfect legs), go for a longer length. Remember, longer lengths, too, have their charms. They're more graceful and they have a certain seductive quality. But bear in mind that too-long skirts look dowdy and too-full skirts appear clumsy.

Finding the Right Skirt

- Go to the designer racks of your local department store to see how skirt linings, pockets, seams, and hems are finished. The better the quality, the more unobtrusive they are. Then, go to the department that fits your price range and choose pieces that come as close as possible to that quality of tailoring and those desired details.

- Make sure pleats are stitched down on a skirt, so they lie flat over the stomach.

- A plain skirt must fall perfectly straight.

- Choose a back zipper over a side zipper for the smoothest-falling line.

- If the waistband doesn't fit or sit right, neither will the skirt!

- Unless you're really skinny, don't buy a skirt with pockets. If you must, keep them stitched closed.

- Make sure fabric is substantial: Too flimsy and every lump and bump shows through; too bulky and you look weighed-down.

- A wrap skirt for the office should be full enough to cover your thighs.

- A back slit, while allowing freedom of movement, should overlap to provide leg coverage. The backs of the knees aren't anyone's most attractive feature.

IF YOU WANT TO MAKE YOUR LEGS LOOK SLIMMER

- Avoid pegged skirts. An A-line style is more slenderizing with heavy legs. The movement of the skirt—whether it's pleated or flared—diverts attention away.

- Camouflage them with color. Match pantyhose and shoes as closely as possible to your skirt. That toned look elongates your silhouette and makes your legs seem slimmer. (You should only wear a pattern if your legs are perfect.)

- Wear a heel that's substantial enough to support the weight of your legs—and is in proportion to your skirt. You're better off with a feminine shoe rather than a clunky one.

PANTS

Pants are an essential part of my working wardrobe, but I know that's not true for every woman. Even though the trend in fashion—as in the corporate world—is toward less uniform dressing, formality still rules in some workplaces and that calls for a skirt.

I wear pants because they're practical—particularly when I'm traveling and when I'm covering fashion shows. Fashion shows are staged to look glamourous to the audience, but backstage they're usually a mess. To interview the designers I often have to scramble up on the runway, climb over lighting and sound

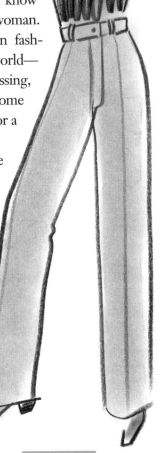

Pleated pant

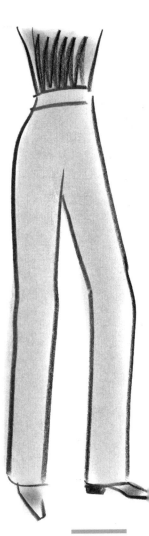

Flat pant

equipment, and get past racks of clothes and benches stacked with accessories. I'm much more agile in pants and I don't constantly risk running my pantyhose. If you have a job where you face similar situations, then consider pants yourself. Two types qualify for business wear: flat pants and pleated trousers. Both styles need dressy, structured tops—jackets or tunics—for professional credibility.

With flat pants you should wear sweaters, tunics, and vests *over* the pants. The flat pants worn with a tunic top create an elongating line, especially when colors are tone-on-tone. With pleated pants, you should tuck sweaters, shirts and blouses in. With either cut, you can wear a jacket.

In a basic working wardrobe, simpler equals more enduring, with pants as well as with skirts.

FINDING THE RIGHT PANTS

- Pockets should be on side seams so they don't add bulk to hips.

- Great basics are pants in rayon or wool crepe, jersey, or gabardine. They are all seasonless fabrics and a good foundation for a wardrobe.

- Find the right length for pants by trying on the shoes you will wear with them. This is essential. Pants that are too short or too long make you look outdated and rob you of presence.

- Pants should hit the top of the heel, so you can see the shape of the shoe and get that elongated line.

- The best shoe for pants is a mid-heel. It takes away from the casual look of the slacks. You have more stance, more authority with a heel.

- If you have a choice, go for pants with a lining. It gives an easier fit and helps hide bulges.

- Whether or not you wear cuffs depends on your height and the width of the pant leg. Tall, lanky types, of course, can carry a smart cuff at any width. If you're under five feet four inches, stay with a straight leg.

- Remember: It takes much less effort to pair a jacket with straight pants than with a skirt.

- Give a special eye to the crotch area: Pulling or bagginess indicates an ill fit and fussing ahead. That's the measurement all good tailors take; it's crucial to a good fit. The best pants always lie smooth and flat.

- Ample seams and hems allow for inevitable weight fluctuations and ever-changing trends.

DRESSES

When mix-and-match sepa-
rates swept in, dresses lost
ground. They've come back
again for two reasons: First, the
fashion industry favors simpler
clothes because they cost less to
manufacture. (Separates generally
cost more to make than dresses.)
Second, working women have
discovered the effortlessness of
the dress. True, it's not as versatile
as a separates outfit, but you can
change the look quite easily with
accessories.

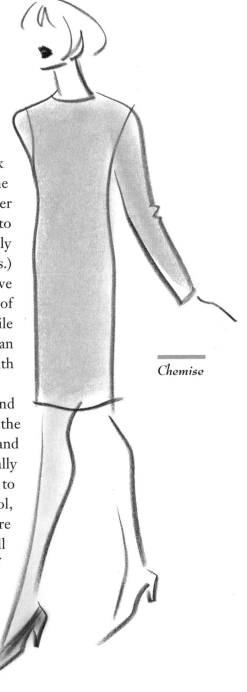

Chemise

The most comfortable and
adaptable style for work is the
chemise. You can dress it up and
down, and it works in practically
every situation from 8 A.M. to
midnight. Solid-color wool,
wool-blend jerseys, or crepes are
the most practical, and they'll
keep their shape better if
they're lined. But chemises in
graphic blocks of colors—

maybe brown, black, and taupe—are also a good value and make a strong statement for important days.

The A-line or trapeze dress—a variation on the chemise—is young, zippy, and a good buy if your weight fluctuates. It's best in a solid color.

Another style that works just as smartly and offers as much day-into-evening wearability as the chemise is the wrap dress. It's softer, more feminine than the chemise, but it functions just as well, effectively hiding figure flaws. It's a natural in solids, but it looks good in quiet prints, too. A wrap dress in a soft abstract print is refreshing when you know you have a grueling day ahead. While giving you authority, it still reminds you that you're a woman.

FINDING THE RIGHT CHEMISE

- The shape of a chemise is so simple, it needs to be well-cut. A soft dress that slides easily over your hips and rear is the most flattering shape.

- Avoid fine fabrics, as they cling. Make sure the fabric is fluid, yet has some body.

- The shoulders set the look for the dress. They must have definition, whether it's soft or strong.

- The best chemise curves in just slightly at the waist, without hugging.

- The cut of a chemise does not allow for a belt unless you're extremely slim—and then the belt must be worn loosely on the hips.

A-line dress

FINDING THE RIGHT WRAP DRESS

- The best wrap dress has a softness of draping for a suggestion of curve.

- Make sure the surplice neckline and skirt are full enough to cover you comfortably.

- Keep hose and shoes monotone for the office. A wrap dress is feminine, and should be played down, not up.

Wrap dress

BLOUSES AND SHIRTS

Blouses and shirts are the collectibles in a wardrobe. The secret to finding the style that best suits you—whether it's collarless, notched-collar, or traditional men's style with a stand that raises the collar to fit snugly—is to consider the shape of your face and the thickness of your neck, as well as the cut of your jackets.

Once you've found your most flattering look, you can buy variations in different fabrics, from cotton knit to lustrous satin.

Plain blouses in your solid or neutral colors are the most useful and compatible because they can easily move around in your wardrobe.

A versatile look—and one of my favorites—is the collarless blouse. I love it for its styling ease. I can drape a scarf over it, add rows of different-size pearls or beads, or wear important earrings and lots of bracelets for different occasions. A collarless blouse has a certain simple geometry that's enormous fun to play with. And fashion *should* be fun!

Wear what gives you pleasure. Clothes should make you feel good, not sensible.

FINDING THE RIGHT COLLARLESS BLOUSE

- Don't clutter up the neckline just because it's plain—that's the beauty of it.

- The collarless blouse looks good with any jacket. And it's just as chic with a collarless jacket as it is by itself.

- Wear a few, well-chosen accessories if you have a short hairstyle—too much bare neck can be unattractive.

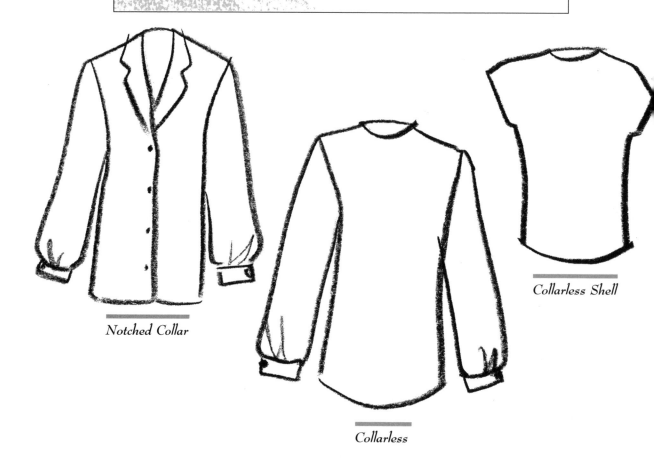

Notched Collar

Collarless

Collarless Shell

FINDING THE RIGHT NOTCHED-COLLAR BLOUSE

- Keep the body of the blouse slim; it must fit the bust but skim the body to be figure-flattering.

- The notched-collar style is soft, meant for crepe and jersey—fabrics that drape. It's the perfect blouse for layering.

- It should look great under a V-necked cardigan, fit comfortably into a skirt or pants, and lie smoothly under a waistband.

- The collar is the focal point so it must be well cut and finely sewn.

- Opt for a pocket only if your bust is small.

- Pay attention to the location of the top button: too high looks uptight, too low reveals too much bra. Don't rely on safety pins—they always show.

- That "V" should flatter your chin and elongate your neck— an especially good choice if your neck is short or thick.

- Consider piping in a contrasting color, and classic patterns—such as dots, foulards, or stripes—to add a fresh note to your wardrobe.

- Cuffs that can be rolled up offer more variety and an easy elegance. With a couple of bracelets, it's a pretty and comfortable look.

FINDING THE RIGHT TRADITIONAL MEN'S SHIRT

• Stretch its function—wear it as a jacket, or layer it over a T-shirt or turtleneck sweater.

Clothes designed by Mario Valentino

• Experiment with the convertible collar. Stand it up around your neck if it's a crisp fabric, or if it's soft, wear it with rows of beads.

• Look for deep armholes for easiest movement.

• Consider length: A shirt should be long enough to stay tucked in even when you're bending and stretching, but not so long that it can't be tucked in neatly.

• Collar and cuffs should have some suppleness. If they're too stiff, they'll be uncomfortable and wear more quickly.

Crisp classic men's shirt

SWEATERS

For work, your best sweater choices are crew necks, turtlenecks, and tunics. Anything too tight will either highlight curves and be too sexy for the office, or show off every lump and bump.

Keep the shapes classic and the fit easy. Tight crew-neck or turtleneck sweaters look uncomfortable and make you hot. They should be slightly loose for a relaxed look. A glimpse of collarbone is feminine.

How you wear a sweater can be a style statement in itself. A smart look is to combine two of the same type of sweater, preferably flat knits, layered over each other—maybe a black crew neck with a little white T-shirt-style sweater peeking out at the neck. If need be, you can peel off one layer and still be stylish.

You can think just as creatively with a twin set—a cardigan and matching shell or crew-neck sweater. Some of the best sweater "ensembles" are those pulled together from an existing wardrobe. Try pairing sweaters in slightly different tones, such as a black cardigan and a very dark grey crew neck. The sweater needn't match the cardigan exactly, but it should be close in tone.

A tank top or bodysuit can be a stylish substitute for the crew neck.

A crew-neck sweater tucked into a skirt or into

Clothes designed by Giorgio Armani

Twin set

trousers cinched with a faux alligator belt is another smart look for the office. In winter, a sweater with a long muffler in a matching or coordinated color looks especially chic. There's also a lovely contrast between the matte look of a sweater and a silk scarf.

FINDING THE RIGHT SWEATER

- A sweater has to be light and well-fitting so it goes easily under suit jackets, cardigans, and shirts. Look for fine flat knits and easy armholes that aren't too low-cut. Anything that bunches up under a jacket ruins the line.

- A sweater should fall two to three inches below your hipbone. It must be long enough to go gracefully over an A-line skirt or tuck neatly into pleated trousers.

- If you like wearing a belt, keep it fairly narrow—one inch or one and a half inches wide. A belt dresses up a sweater and skirt, and if they're all the same shade they'll look like a dress.

- Don't tuck a sweater into a flat skirt or trousers; blouse it over for a sense of ease.

- Choose blends that come as close to the look of cashmere as possible.

- De-fuzz pills. It takes just seconds to freshen up sweaters. You can buy a machine for just a few dollars.

- Buy the softest yarns you can afford and the most classic stitches. Ribs, cables and flat weaves are timeless choices.

COATS

The most versatile modern coat is a seven-eighths length, which works with most figure types. You can wear it over short and long skirts as well as pants, and it looks just as right for evening as it does for day.

If you have only enough in your clothing allowance to buy one coat, make it a seven-eighths length. Many styles come in this length; anoraks, belted short trenches, wraps, and cape-coats are traditionally good buys.

The second choice—especially if you're tall—is a long greatcoat: a trench, a wrap, or a bathrobe style. If you're small, choose a greatcoat that comes to just below midcalf. Any other length tends to look dated and overpowering.

Whatever your choice, it should be easy and loose. Few things look worse than a skimpy, ill-fitting coat.

Modern coats are made to go over everything, and should have a certain nonchalant style, a casual sophistication, an air of throwaway luxury.

Clothes designed by Oscar de la Renta

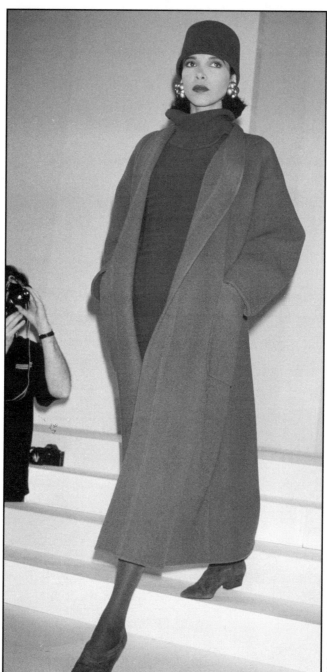

Greatcoat

Clothes designed by Oscar de la Renta

FINDING THE RIGHT COAT

- A modern coat should never be too formal. Fitted and uptight are outdated.

- Function comes first. Keep your climate in mind when choosing the weight of the coat.

- A coat should button high at the neck for warmth, but look equally good unbuttoned.

- The best coat is multifunctional and works just as well over pants and skirts as it does over dresses.

- Buy the best fabric you can afford. It should be soft and supple to keep you looking slim and shapely.

- A coat should be cut to look smart when it's worn fully open.

- Sleeves should be long, preferably to just below the wrist bone.

- Beware of too many details, especially on a trench coat: You don't need an excess of buttons, buckles, or epaulets.

- A zip-out lining gives a coat greater versatility, but watch out for bulkiness when you belt it.

- The best wrap either falls straight or tapers slightly to the hem.

- Shoulder pads should be as small as possible. Remember, you'll be layering your coat over jackets and sweaters.

4

Building a Wardrobe for Business Travel

In today's business world, a heavy travel schedule is routine for many of the successful executives I know.

I also travel extensively for work. The big trips are to Europe and Japan to cover the showings of the fall and spring collections—a whirl-wind schedule running from shows to press parties to dinners. In between I do quite a bit of domestic traveling to give talks about the design world. The basis of any successful travel wardrobe—business or pleasure—is in the organization. It's key in helping to reduce the stress of travel.

The pleasure of any trip at all is traveling light. You are always under much less pressure if you don't have a lot of things to worry about, including what you're going to wear that evening or the next day. The secret is to list every function and meeting you will have to attend. Then work out the *minimum* number of items needed to dress appropriately for each one. I say *minimum*, because too many clothes will confuse you when you're tired and busy. Your suitcase will be heavier than it has to be and you'll waste time packing and unpacking.

The type of wardrobe you take depends on the nature of your trip. You'll need more outfits for six days in one city than for three days each in two cities. (Different people would see you in the two places so you could wear exactly the same things twice.)

I start my trip-wardrobe plan by roughly listing the clothes I'll need for the various functions I've scheduled. This takes seconds—I do it in my diary during a taxi ride. And I usually start planning a week or two in advance in case anything needs to be cleaned, pressed, or repaired. I check the list a few times to see that I have all I need. I find I enjoy the

process more if I let the list percolate in my mind for a few days rather than making instant decisions.

A few days before the trip I get out my folding rack and hang the clothes on it. (The rack cost me about $25 a dozen years ago and is one of my best investments ever.) Then I add the accessories, starting with shoes and bags, and work up through belts and jewelry. (I keep all shoes, belts, and bags in the same color so they're interchangeable. Then I don't have to give a second's thought as to whether or not they "go.")

The next day, I start to edit. Often I remove half the pieces I've selected. Seeing the clothes on the rack helps me to figure out how I can cut down on basic items like skirts, pants, shoes.

This system—whether the trip is for three days or three weeks—is practically foolproof for me. I rarely forget essentials. I always travel light. And I often discover new combinations. But most important, it doesn't take too much time and I get a lot of pleasure from it.

WHAT TO TAKE

You'll want to choose the simplest pieces, ones that you know fit you easily and comfortably: dresses, jackets, skirts, pants, and tunics.

I'd rather take a thick pair of pantyhose than pack a heavy skirt.

New clothes are *not* for trips! You don't need the stress of finding a brand-new jacket is too tight or really doesn't go with your basic skirt.

Of course you can experiment with new accessories, but include some of your favorites as well— the ones that give you an instant lift when you're tired.

Your best bet for the actual traveling is a neutral-colored, wrinkle-proof pantsuit. Lighten the look with a white shell and a lively scarf. You're then prepared for the worst—delays, rerouting, changes in weather—and more than likely you'll arrive looking great.

Carry a light coat. Then, if it's a short trip you're already wearing half your wardrobe. If you put the rest in a garment bag, you won't even have to check your luggage.

THE FLIGHT ITSELF

However long the flight, certain staples will help keep you comfortable.

Your bag should be large enough to carry chewing gum or sugar-free candy, a book to read, and your diary. It should also have a pocket large enough to carry your passport, traveler's checks, and credit

cards. It's a good idea to photo-copy these before you go. Leave one copy at home for your records and carry another copy in your suitcase.

The bag you carry on should also contain a small bag for pills (pain reliever and any spe-cial medication), hand lotion, and a tiny mister to spray your face with water. It's most refreshing in the dry air of a plane.

All of these things make it easier for you to smile your way through a trip, no matter what goes wrong. I've found that airline staff often seem tired and har-ried. If you complain angrily you get nowhere. If you smile, the results can be most gratifying.

Trench coat

THREE BASICS FOR THE PLANE AND AFTER

Lightweight raincoat in a dark tone, black or pale neutral. Of course, taupe, navy, camel, black, and beige are standbys. It should be light and soft enough so it packs in a minimum of space and wrinkles fall out when you unroll it.

Big challis wool shawl to throw over a light top in restaurants, planes, or cars, for a little extra warmth. Deep red or burgundy is a good choice if it works with your skin tone: Both colors look good with most other colors. Also it should be lightweight and easy to pack.

Low-to-mid-heel slip-on shoes that are old friends. However long the delays or the trudge from gate to gate, you can walk in comfort. This is as good for your face as it is for your feet.

Basics for a Three-Day Business Trip:

• Grey (or taupe, beige, or camel) wool knit pantsuit

• Grey, black, and white plaid jacket

• Black gabardine straight skirt

• Grey sweater

• Pale grey tunic

• White crew-neck shell

You travel in the grey pantsuit and white blouse, mix and match them with the skirt and plaid jacket for day. At night wear the grey tunic or white blouse with the black skirt or grey pants.

"Suit" separates

BASICS FOR A SEVEN-TO-TEN-DAY BUSINESS TRIP

To the preceding three-day list add:

A simple sleeveless grey dress that can be worn with the plaid jacket for day, or with a pretty print shawl for evening.

A black jacket that can team with the black gabardine skirt for a suit look, for day or evening.

Black knit pants that go with the plaid jacket for day, or with a pale grey tunic or white blouse for nighttime.

Sleeveless sheath dress

DOs & DON'Ts FOR BUSINESS TRAVEL

DO buy a suitcase in a neutral color that looks businesslike. Canvas with leather straps is a classic.

DO plan to hand-wash clothes. It saves on suitcase space as well as wear and tear and dry-cleaning expense. To speed drying time, wrap rinsed clothes tightly in a dry towel to absorb the excess water, then hang to dry.

DO get up and walk around as often as you can when you're making a long trip in a plane, car, or train. The movement will aid circulation and help prevent cramping.

DO try to limit your luggage to, say, a garment bag, a carry-on duffel, and one suitcase (best if it can be stored overhead, so you can disembark quickly).

DO apply a superhydrating lotion (sometimes called "flight cream") to your face once airborne. Reapply it on a long flight.

DON'T forget to pack a few essentials—a change of underwear, toothbrush and toothpaste—in your carry-on bag or tote. Then you won't need to scramble to replace them should your luggage get lost.

DON'T leave home without making a quick list of the most important things you've packed—to use in case you have to report a missing suitcase and file a claim.

DON'T wear anything for air travel but the most comfortable clothes and shoes. On a long flight your waist and feet tend to swell.

DON'T forget to do your exercise routine. Exercising makes you aware of your body, and you'll be less likely to overeat at receptions and dinners.

DON'T ever forget that travel is exhausting. In addition to the flight itself, you have to deal with the luggage, the crowds, and confusion at the airport. So don't push yourself, and rest when you can.

IF YOU CAN
AFFORD ONLY
ONE BUSINESS-
TRIP ESSENTIAL,
MAKE IT . . .
A great tote bag
that holds all your
necessities and is not
too heavy.

Pantsuit and tote

Clothes-Packing Tips

- Use plastic dry-cleaner bags to keep clothes from getting crushed. Cut the bags into shapes suitable for blouses, sweaters, etc. Then fold the clothes over the bags. You'll find they trap enough air to prevent wrinkling. And pack extras; they come in handy for storing wet bathing suits and dirty laundry.

- In some cases—with knit pants, for example—it's easier to roll the pants and plastic together. This takes up less room and is a guarantee against creases.

- Put shoes in plastic bags. I sometimes put gloves or pantyhose in bags, too. It makes them easier to find. When I unpack I don't remove the bags until I'm ready to wear what's in them.

- Fold along permanent or "set" creases (in pant legs, shirtsleeves, etc.) whenever possible. This encourages the "fresh from the dry cleaner" look and cuts down on ironing.

- Tissue paper is another secret weapon against wrinkles. Line each garment with paper, then fold lengthwise in thirds (to correspond with the body's natural "creases": elbows, waist, knees).

- Pack the heaviest items on the bottom layer to prevent everything else from wrinkling, the most crushable items on top.

- Hang up clothes as soon as you reach your destination. If they're wrinkled, hang them in the bathroom, turn the hot water on in the shower, and steam them.

- Should you need to take hangers along, the inflatable kind (available in travel stores) take up almost no space and weigh next to nothing!

- Pack what you need to wear first on top, so there's no need to search if you have an appointment immediately after you arrive at your destination.

- If you don't have a travel iron or steamer (another smart investment), you can usually get one from the hotel.

COSMETICS-PACKING TIPS

- Collect sample sizes of your favorite skin-care and makeup products (fragrance, too) before your trip. When you buy a beauty product, ask for samples for your travel kit. Check out drugstores for inexpensive, trial-size beauty aids, such as toothpaste, shampoo, conditioner, and deodorant.

- To keep luggage as lightweight as possible, carry pills and creams in plastic containers. Count out the number of pills or capsules you'll need for the days you'll be away and put them in labeled containers.

- Plastic makeup organizers with compartments are wonderful for sorting essentials, from lipsticks to cosmetic brushes. Make sure the lining is plastic, too, for the easiest cleanup should a spill occur.

- Carry your cosmetics on board with you. They'll keep better at cabin temperature than in the cargo hold where extreme cold or heat can ruin formulations. And they'll be handy when you want to reapply them.

- Streamline your makeup choices with double-duty products, such as cream-to-powder base, eyeshadow that pinch-hits as liner, lip pencil that fills in like lipstick, blush that highlights eyes, too. A suntan product with aloe vera also makes an excellent body moisturizer.

- Make sure cosmetics are "cushioned" (those plastic bags create protective pockets of air) to prevent breakage and leakage. To further safeguard against spillage from plastic bottles (shampoo, moisturizer, etc.), compress the open bottle, cover the opening with plastic wrap and then close the top while continuing to squeeze the bottle.

- Keep sharp-edged beauty aids (razor, scissors, etc.) encased.

- For easiest access, pack all-of-a-kind essentials together, in separate bags—toothbrush, toothpaste, dental floss, and mouthwash; feminine hygiene products; shampoo, conditioner, hair spray.

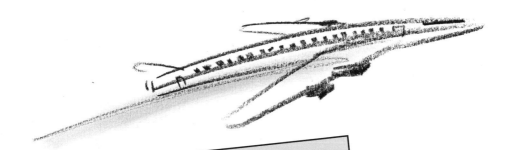

LONG-FLIGHT <u>MUST-HAVES</u>

- ✔ Water mister
- ✔ Toothbrush and toothpaste
- ✔ Good-luck charm
- ✔ Eye drops
- ✔ Two-way mirror
- ✔ Nail file
- ✔ Cleansing and moisturizing creams
- ✔ Talcum powder

5

Building a Wardrobe for Evening

Most successful women have a busy night life—whether it's filled with job-related engagements, or strictly social events. Because of my line of work, my evenings are very full. I'll have at least a couple of parties, openings, or dinners every night of the week in the fashion world. I can't accept every invitation, but news-worthy events are a must. On top of the must attend work events, my husband and I like to go out, see friends, and entertain.

Like most stylish women, I couldn't cope with it all if I hadn't built my evening wardrobe around separates. And I must say, I get more pleasure from these outfits than I do from my working wardrobe. My fantasy life comes more into play in this aspect of my dress—there's more romance, more drama, and even greater elegance. I find this change of pace, this fulfilled expression of my "other self," enables me to achieve more of what I want in my working life—success!

LOOKS FOR EVENING

The key to success in evening looks is to build on your daytime wardrobe. Collecting separates in the same basic colors will enable you to create the greatest number of outfits. If you keep them all in your chosen neutrals—black, grey, beige, brown, navy—and stay with seasonless fabrics, they'll give you unlimited mileage year-round.

> EVENING WARDROBE BASICS
> Short crepe skirt
> Flowing soft-crepe pajama pants
> Long drop-pleat skirt
> Tapered or straight pants

Then you can team dressy separates with your daytime pieces when you go straight from the job to a party or dinner. A shimmery white or ivory stretch satin bodysuit under a neutral jacket makes it instantly evening. Add jewelry, a ribbon in your hair, a small clutch bag, and off you go.

BEST EVENING FABRICS

Matte jersey

Silky knit jersey

Georgette

Matte or silky crepe

Satin

Velvet

Organza

Chiffon

BOTTOMS—SKIRTS AND PANTS

Bottom separates should be foundation pieces that have a dozen lives.

At most evening functions you're either standing in a crowded room or sitting down, so what's on top is in focus. You can get by with just two bottoms in your basic color—a short skirt and a pair of wide pants. These are almost as dressy as a long skirt and look more modern. Once you have these mainstays, you can add a long skirt—any length from midcalf to floor—and straight or tapered pants.

Fabrics should be dressy—crepe, satin, velvet, matte, or silky jersey. Shapes should be simple, with few, if any, details.

Evening fashion should be fun. Part of the enjoyment of a party should be planning to look your best.

The best skirts are straight, A-line, or bias-cut and have half-inch belts.

The best pants have an inch-wide waistband with loops, and pockets on the side seams. Narrow pants should be flat across the top and taper gently to the ankle. Wide pants should get their fullness from deep pleats at the waist. If you're tall, the waistband can be two inches. The width of the pants allows for a wide, dramatic belt or sash.

Once you have the basics you can start adding more glamorous pieces—a short sequined skirt, tapered pants in pale or jewel colors, or wide pants in soft floaty fabrics.

TOPS

From the simplest metallic tank to the long, see-through georgette tunic, tops are collectibles. Buy them in your most flattering basic color so you can also team them with your daytime clothes and get extra mileage. A shimmery silver blouse tied at the waist over grey flannel pants can go out to dinner in seconds. Add drop earrings, bracelets, and silver sandals for an easy, yet elegant effect. Tone-on-tone dressing is not only more luxurious, it's more slimming.

Clothes designed by Donna Karan

Soft full pants

FIVE OF THE BEST TOPS OF ALL TIME

Man's-style shirt in white organza. Make it crisp if you're dramatic; soft if you're romantic.

See-through georgette tunic in peachy-pink. You must find a good flesh-toned bodysuit to wear beneath it. Go to a dance or ballet outfitter's shop.

Metallic tank top with pants. It's perfect for summer day-into-evening.

Simple red halter top in jersey. It goes under suits and always looks great. It could be silk or fine wool jersey, depending on how dressy you want to be.

Black lace crew-neck bodysuit —with a satin belt or jet beads, you can play up the textures in the lace.

Clothes designed by Byblos

**Shimmery halter
wrap top**

Then go all out for color—brights, lights, and, of course, metallics. Remember, the three most glamorous colors for evening are red, pink, and white (red for attention, pink to flatter the skin, and white to catch the light).

Each top you buy should work with at least two of your bottoms.

The best fabrics are wrinkle-proof—knits (from jersey to metallic), brocades, embroideries, sequins, and lace. They're all elegant, and they can easily stand up to a night of partying and dancing.

THE LITTLE BLACK DRESS

There is, of course, no greater staple than the little black dress. In the right style it's timeless, extremely versatile, and takes up no closet space. For most of this century, it has been the mainstay in the evening wardrobe of the fashionable woman.

The little black dress originated in the 1920s, in Paris, at the couture. There were many variations, and each was beautifully cut and looked like a little jewel. So remember that when you put one on, it's not a play-safe dress—it's meant to be daring and dramatic. You should try to make it as upbeat and as individual as you possibly can.

Because there are so many little black dresses

The little black dress

IF YOU CAN AFFORD ONLY ONE FABULOUS EVENING LOOK, MAKE IT A . . . *Little black dress.* It'll see you through countless evening parties and special occasions. And if you go for an asymmetrical length and strong jewelry you can even wear it to a formal event.

around, choose one with pizzazz to make you stand out: short and sexy with rows of swingy fringe, or with an offbeat asymmetrical hemline. Or buy one in a classic, but not too covered-up style and change the look with accessories. This takes practice—a few hours on a rainy Saturday afternoon—but it's well worth the effort.

I always have a couple of black midcalf dresses in my wardrobe: one in jersey, the other in crepe, my two favorite fabrics for evening. I accessorize them in several ways. When I rush home to dress for a party, I simply choose one or the other, slip it on, and take off for the evening.

When I have to go out for the evening straight from work, I add a touch of glitter to a little black dress—usually it can be a sequined scarf. It's about the easiest thing to put on, and the metallic gleam and the change of texture play up the strikingly simple black backdrop. Each season I change my personal touches—my signature accents—to give the dresses a fresh, updated look.

There are three points to remember when accessorizing your little black dress. First, black on black is an extremely sophisticated way to go, and

TIPS FOR BUYING A LITTLE BLACK DRESS

- Carefully consider hem length: One that falls mid-calf or just above the knee offers the most timeless look, and one that's suitable for most occasions. A micromini, for instance, wouldn't give you as much mileage.

- Always try it on with sheer black pantyhose and the heels you plan to wear with it—before handing over your charge card.

- Once you've bought your black dress, check your shoes, bags, and underpinnings to make sure everything works, and take time to accessorize it perfectly. Then it will be waiting for you the second you want it.

- If you fall in love with a dress that's more daring than your usual choices but looks *fabulous* on you, don't rationalize your purchase—just buy it. It'll give you a glow every time you put it on and that's worth plenty.

*Midcalf-length
little black dress*

Clothes designed by Isaac Mizrahi

you'll have fun mixing different shades—matte and shiny, for instance, is a striking combination. You can add another texture with a velvet bow in your hair, or a sequined belt or flower—again, keeping it all in black.

The second way to go is with a brilliant dash of color, such as red, emerald, blue, or gold. It can be a marvelous hat, headband, or pair of gloves, the most beautiful sandals or handbag, or even a pretty silk shawl draped casually around your shoulders.

Third, you can mix black with metallics. Silver and gold were made for each other, but so were gold and black. The warm metallic tone sparks black's sophistication, yielding a rich, stunning contrast. Or try silver and black for a vastly different effect. The shimmery cool light of silver is a perfect foil for deep, dark black.

If you can't wear black, choose another deep color for your basic dress. Dark red, cognac, and midnight blue are all versatile and flattering colors.

*Black on black:
matte on shine*

Clothes designed by Isaac Mizrahi

ADD YOUR OWN KIND OF DAZZLE

With understated evening separates, it takes only one elegant extra—like the glitter and glamour of a jeweled jacket—to project your individuality and style. A beaded or sequined classic-shape jacket that goes over a dress, skirt, or top and pants is a wardrobe essential for most of the stylish women I know.

Some have saved up to buy it, realizing it's a piece they will have for the rest of their lives. They wear it year after year to formal occasions, changing the look by teaming it with different separates. One season it might be a short skirt; another year, pajama pants. It could even be worn with bike shorts. Some years, when fashion has been overglitzed, you might want to retire your jeweled jacket. But treat it like a friend who's gone off for a visit and welcome it back.

If you can't afford a jacket, look for a jeweled sweater or cardigan. It's been called the "anytime sweater," adaptable enough to go over jeans as well as an evening skirt, pants, or leggings. Choose your sweater carefully. Make sure it's the right length for your proportions.

It's your personality, aided by your clothes, that attracts people.

It shouldn't be too fitted; a straighter-line version will always be in fashion.

Look for equally chic accessories that add a surprise twist to simple styles—perhaps an exotic-print scarf, a velvet collar, or an embroidered vest. They're the kind of touches that define a signature look.

COVER-UPS

The most modern cover-up for evening is a huge triangular or U-shaped shawl in wool or cashmere. It wraps around your body, and rarely slips, giving you warmth as well as dash. It's best in a neutral color: black, burgundy, bitter brown, or bright red. In summer, something as sheer as a chiffon wrap can protect you from air conditioning with an alluring effect. Also consider a knit lace wrap. As it falls open, the look changes, and it can be romantic or sophisticated, depending on your choice of pattern.

U-shaped cashmere shawl

Clothes designed by Donna Karan

AT-HOME DRESSING

Being well-dressed should be as important when you're entertaining at home as when you go out. The most celebrated party givers I know always look their most glamorous for their guests. They keep the color scheme of their decor in mind when choosing at-home clothes. This doesn't mean wearing pale blue to match the walls. It means wearing a color that has a similar depth of tone—whether it's in yellow, pink, or green. This tends to make the hostess appear at ease, and helps set a relaxed atmosphere.

Pants and tops are comfortable for entertaining at home. They allow you freedom of movement when you're cooking or serving. Two looks to consider are a long dress or caftan that will make you feel and appear more elegant. (One of the best places to look for them is in the cover-ups or swimwear department.) There are many variations and your figure should decide the way you go.

A tunic and slim pull-on pants create a stylish option if you've got bulges to hide. When the two pieces are in different fabrics, the effect is especially attractive. The contrast of textures is more modern and it doesn't look so much like loungewear. And if you keep your pants in a basic neutral—such

as black, grey, or navy—then you'll be able to switch just your tunic tops.

Another variation would be full pants or pleated trousers and a pretty body-fitting stretch top or sweater. That way, when you reach out to serve something, you don't risk ruining your blouse. Of course, if you prefer a skirt, substitute a flattering style for the pants.

Be careful with accessories when you're entertaining. When you're serving food, belts with large, ornate buckles can be uncomfortable, and swinging pendants and bracelets can get in the way.

Another look for evening—whether entertaining at home or going out—is the jumpsuit. Being in one color, neck to ankle, is always slimming. The jumpsuit has a great graphic quality that projects style, and the simple shape lends itself to varied accessorizing. Beads at the neck—as many as you dare—are good. Or, for a change, try dangling earrings and brightly colored sandals or ballet slippers. (Since ballet slippers are so inexpensive, you can afford to get them in silver or gold, and black.) A jumpsuit in a softly draped style can go to practically any formal function if you add dressy accessories—particularly your bag and sandals. It always looks younger and more modern than a long dress.

If you can't wear a jumpsuit, a blouse tucked

into pajama pants will create a similar effect. Keep the fabrics and colors as close as possible, and cinch the waist with a suede belt. Suede has many gradations of color and will help create the illusion that your top and bottom match.

Incidentally, when you're going to a party at someone else's home, wear your prettiest color. It will help his or her home look more festive. Save your little black dress for cocktail parties, restaurants, and the theater—occasions for appearing chic rather than feminine.

Dressing well

gets you all the attention

you need.

THREE WAYS TO ACCESSORIZE A JUMPSUIT

• Fill in the neckline with strands of pearls, beads, and necklaces, and put on pretty shoes.

• Slip on a great headband that matches a belt. (Make sure the belt width is no more than two inches; any wider and it'll cut your figure and height in half.)

• Make wrists interesting with wide cuffs and bracelets, and simply add earrings.

(And don't forget that important *unseen* accessory that can do so much for the slimming quality of the jumpsuit: small shoulder pads. If your shoulders are rounded or sloped, pads provide the lift needed to put things in proper proportion.)

Jumpsuit-look separates and cover-up

6

Building a Wardrobe
for Leisure

While your work clothes must be kept under control, at leisure you can relax, experiment, and be innovative. This is the time to indulge your sense of fashion and fun, and let your fantasies fly high. Many successful businesswomen I know tap into their private visions of themselves and express that inner being in their weekend wear. It makes them feel

Tap into your fantasy…

and let your private-time wardrobe reflect it. Not only do you learn more about yourself but you become a more interesting person to your husband and your friends.

more feminine, and enables them to have a healthier outlook when it comes to work.

In my private life, I'm a wife—not a television personality. On weekends, I want to be softer, more romantic.

My fantasy in the summer is to look as though I just stepped out of an F. Scott Fitzgerald novel wearing Gatsby-style long skirts and gently flowing chiffon scarves. It's a side of me I can't show the world during the week because of my job, but I can live it during the weekend.

In winter, the fantasy changes: I pretend I'm very modern. I like sleek grey knits and bold silver jewelry. I wear catsuits or unitards under long tunic sweaters and stride out in thick-soled walking shoes and a shearling jacket. It makes me feel like I'm ready for the twenty-first century.

I don't spend a lot of money indulging my fantasies. I just collect things along the way. Not everything I have works on the job, but a lot of the pieces will.

WEEKEND WEAR

The activewear revolution, driven by fabric technology, has forever blurred the boundary between exercisewear and everyday clothes, and for good

DOs & DON'Ts FOR A LEISURE WARDROBE

DO look at your leisure wardrobe as a total coordinated package.

DO keep to your basic colors.

DO try to have it so carefully thought-out you never have to worry about unexpected invitations.

DO have some fun with separates in stretch fabrics. They get better every season.

DO look for quality when buying separates, from T-shirts to snow boots.

DON'T get stuck wearing the same look over and over again.

DON'T buy anything without trying it on first!

DON'T buy anything that's difficult to maintain.

DON'T save anything that's shrunk or ripped beyond repair.

DON'T overaccessorize: Let your outfit and a few choice pieces of jewelry have their impact.

Catsuit

Clothes designed by Donna Karan

reason. Activewear performs. It keeps you warm in cold weather and cool when it's hot. And it keeps you unencumbered in ways that fashion never could before.

These sleek, stretchy, high-function looks are the basis for a modern leisure wardrobe. They're lightning dressing—they go on *fast*. Natural and synthetic fibers and blends that are knit in the simplest shapes can be worn by themselves or with other pieces for the easiest way of dressing the century's ever seen.

Start with the basics—bodysuits, leotards, bra tops, leggings, bike shorts—and you can quickly add on other pieces. A T-shirt, sweater, jacket, pair of jeans, even a loose-fitting dress, are all perfect for layering on top of these basics. Unlike its bulky, shapeless predecessor, sweats, today's activewear lets a sense of the body show through, even if a big sweater, shirt, or dress covers most of it.

Increasingly, these pieces—once categorized only as innerwear—are being worn as outerwear. The look is informal, and certainly not meant for the office. But that's not to say a bodysuit can't go to work. Partnered with the right career clothes—under a jacket, cardigan sweater, or shirt—a bodysuit earns respectability for nine-to-five wear.

Carry your style through— by means of your colors and personal preferences—to each aspect of your life.

MAKE MODERN FIBERS YOUR FIRST CHOICE

This activewear revolution is one that's been gaining momentum for twenty years, and it's definitely going to be a major influence in the future. The technology of fabrics is continuing to grow and it will affect what you wear and how you wear your clothes. More and more, garments will be able to perform—that is, they'll be functional as well as fashionable.

VARIETY OF ACTIVEWEAR FABRICS . . .

Velour
Velvet
Salt-and-pepper tweeds
Abstract and floral prints
Space-dyed
Corduroy
Lace
Heathered cotton

Intentionally-crushed fabrics are eliminating the need for ironing. And after impacting on hosiery, stretch fibers such as nylon/Lycra/spandex and Supplex®, and microfibers such as Micromattique® and MicroSupreme®, are lending greater flexibility and ease to leisure clothes than ever before. These miracle fibers are taking over as *the* most comfortable, colorful, and elegant way to dress in off-hours.

The big reason for comfort is the spandex. It's being paired with nylon, cotton, and even polyester,

Sweater and straight
trousers

Clothes designed by Hermes

making them all easy-care. Leisure wardrobes built on these fabrics are modern, convenient, maintenance-free, and certainly packable.

On the style side, activewear yarns are being spun to imitate the most luxurious fabrics—many are as sumptuous as the finest silk—and in the most delicious colors. (They're also being printed, and lined in fleece for extra warmth.)

To help you in your color choices, many manufacturers are now offering sportswear lines that coordinate with their basic exercise pieces.

RESORT

Many of your at-home clothes can be put in your resort suitcase, but you *do* need special things to perk up your wardrobe and make life more fun. Keep to your basic neutrals and your proportions, and your choices will work across the board for you.

Now, however, is the time to buy accessories that totally change the mood—things that you would never wear at home. If you're heading for the sun, buy espadrilles, colorful scarves, rope (or hemp) belts, brightly and boldly printed shirts, a long sundress, a great woven straw hat . . . and more whimsical accessories, such as a shell bracelet.

DOs & DON'Ts FOR HOLIDAY TRAVEL

DO put sunscreens, tissues, and combs in a separate soft bag so you'll find them easily when you're heading for the pool or beach.

DO put all your cosmetics and hair accessories in separate, clear plastic bags so you can keep them visible and accessible in the bathroom.

DO take off metal jewelry before going through the airport metal detector. It's quicker and easier than being stopped.

DO take out contact lenses before boarding a long flight. Keep them secure, but handy.

DO board the plane early: You'll be sure of your seat—a good start for avoiding the stress of the holiday crush—plus you'll find more space for storage.

DO smile all the way through boarding. You'll get into the holiday spirit sooner.

DON'T forget a pretty scarf or hat to protect your hair from the sun. Harmful rays bleach hair and that can be a real headache if your hair is already colored.

DON'T carry a lot of hand luggage, however many souvenirs you buy. Storage space on planes is scarce and it's often a long walk through the terminal, even if you don't have to pass through customs.

DON'T arrive at your destination looking ragged. Make up on the plane minutes before landing. You've worked hard for this holiday, so get ready to make the most of your investment—and time.

If you're going where there's snow, treat yourself to a cozy shearling hat and gloves, colorful thick socks, a rugged leather belt bag. You'll use them again and again, and not only when you're on holiday.

These types of things also help transform your outlook. By putting them on, you'll get into the spirit of your vacation faster.

Another way to get into the mood is with self-tanning cream. It may not be as perfect as you'd like, but it's better than unevenly colored skin (especially against a bathing suit). And it's better than tanning yourself for real.

Some final advice: Tone everything so it all goes well together. Then there's less confusion—and more room in your suitcase.

Shirt and city shorts

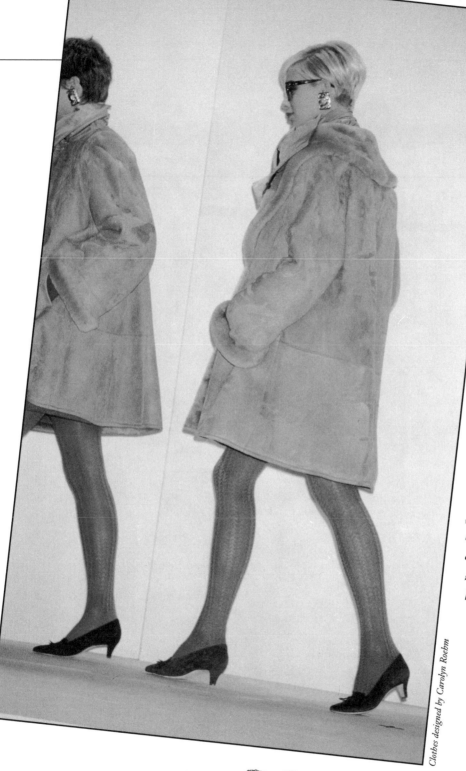

Clothes designed by Carolyn Roehm

*Shearling
coat in
seven-eighths
length*

BASICS TO CONSIDER FOR A RESORT WEEK

This is what I pack when I'm off on holiday. You can follow the same list or modify it, depending upon what you have in your wardrobe. You really can't go wrong mixing and matching these basics. Then it's time to have fun!

- Great black-and-white or tan-and-white checked jacket that goes sporty or casual

- Four top-quality T-shirts (extras to layer if it's cold; to change if it's hot and sticky)

- Knit cardigan or lightweight sweater

- Tank top

- White cotton shirt

- Black silk shirt

- Jumpsuit

- Bareback sleeveless chemise

- Black knit dress

- Pajama top and pants

- White tie-waist pants

- Black leggings or blue jeans

- Long, flowing washed-silk skirt

- City shorts or simple skirt

- Bike shorts

- Black maillot

- Pareo

- Long black shawl

- Open-weave hat

- Sneakers (in case you go on a boat)

- Flip-flops

FOR HOT CLIMATES

Dress standards at different islands and resorts vary, so ask your travel agent. If you can wear a sarong and tank top to dinner, then you needn't pack as much. On a cruise, however, you'll dress up every night for dinner, so you'll need to take as many changes as possible.

Natural fibers such as linen, cotton, and silk are always your best choice for the tropics because they breathe. Linen maintains its elegant appeal even when it's slightly rumpled. Cotton can be hand-washed, then hung out to dry, returning to crisp condition the next morning. And there's nothing as sensuous as silk on a balmy tropical night.

The more loose-fitting the garment, the more comfortable you'll be. (Stretch separates made with nylon can lock in moisture, leaving you feeling soggy.) But that

SIX HOT-WEATHER LIFESAVERS

White cotton shirt, long-sleeved, with a collar.

Sandals in a neutral brown.

Wide-brimmed straw hat that you can anchor with a scarf.

Sunscreen—a must every morning for your face and backs of hands.

Classic sunglasses, light and comfortable.

Lightweight cotton scarf to safeguard the back of your neck against burning; you can also mop your brow with it or wrap it around your head to get your sticky hair off your face.

T-shirt and loose wrap skirt

Clothes designed by Michael Kors

Clothes designed by Ralph Lauren

doesn't mean restricting yourself to oversized caftans. Swingy little trapeze dresses, sleeveless vests that double as tops, men's shirts, abbreviated flared skirts—these styles move away from the body instead of encasing it, generating a tiny breeze with every step you take. Look for details that are deliciously cooling, and the weather will never do you in. Open weaves, cutouts, and slits are as good as air-conditioning on a sultry day.

"THE BEST REVIVER when you come back from the beach hot and sticky is to *run cold water over your wrists*. It's calming as well as cooling."

SWIMWEAR

How to Buy the Most Flattering Style

The first thing to look for is a comfortable, well-fitting suit with inner construction that best flatters your figure.

If you're slim and athletic, you'll need a simple tank with, perhaps, sewn-in cups to give you a little support. If you're small-busted, look for light padding, draping across the chest, or a strategically placed pattern to visually build up your bustline.

If you're overendowed, you must look at power-net lining, underwires, soft or foam padding, or hard cups. Try on different suits, and you'll find one of these will fit you and give you an attractive shape.

Also look for different necklines—from square-shaped to mock surplice—for a more pleasing effect. To protect the upper chest from exposure to the sun, many swimsuit manufacturers are now making high-necked styles. This could be the perfect solution for you.

If tummy bulge is a figure challenge, look for a suit that's draped across the middle. The soft flow of the fabric will help disguise any roundness.

Or maybe your thighs are a sore spot for you. A suit that's cut high on the legs will make your legs look longer and the curve of your thighs less obvious. A skirted look can also prove to be a pretty distraction.

*Figure-flattering
color-blocked
swimsuits*

Clothes designed by Bill Blass

If your figure is perfect, you can wear any style of swimsuit. A bikini with a bandeau top and matching bottom will show off a lot, yet it won't reveal *everything*. A racer tank swimsuit with a hint of shine will also look stunning, as that shimmer will highlight your curves.

Make the most of your beautiful figure by choosing a color that attracts attention. The most flattering is white, white, white—especially if you have a suntan.

Finding the Right Fit

The right fit is as important as the right style. There's nothing worse than fussing with a suit that doesn't quite cover your breasts or bottom.

My cardinal rule is: If it's not comfortable, don't buy it. The suit you can wear without a second's thought is the one you'll be happiest in and the least self-conscious about.

To ensure a proper fit, the bra cups must completely cover the breasts. Look out for any gaping or flattening; they're signs of a bad fit. If there are straps, they should be adjustable, with enough length so they don't cut into your shoulders.

To determine if a suit fits across your bottom, you'll need to stand, sit, and bend before a three-way mirror. Observe how high the suit rides (if at all) in

> *If a swimsuit isn't comfortable, don't buy it. There's nothing worse than fussing with it.*

back when you change positions. Ideally, it should stay put, providing full coverage.

If you're buying a two-piece style, the same rules apply. But do make sure the waist sits where it belongs. If it falls short, it'll look as awkward as it feels.

How Patterns Can Make You Look Better

If your weight is a concern, consider a patterned suit. Many swimwear designers take size into account when they choose the fabrics for the suits.

The first to try: vertical stripes. Designers sometimes cut them in unusual ways or in different widths, and they work wonders for an overweight shape.

If you're heavy, avoid large floral or abstract prints, as they will only call attention to your size. But smaller prints worn on the slimmest parts of your body can reshape your figure in the most complementary way. A suit that combines a pretty, small-scale print with all-purpose, slimming black is truly figure-forgiving.

Color-blocking in graphic patterns is also worth considering. The right one can "resculpt" your figure, visually paring inches from your torso. If your thighs need slimming or your waist needs whittling, strategically placed color panels can do the trick.

COVER-UPS

The easiest and most stylish way to cover up is with a pareo—a square of fabric that is at least 72" x 72". It can be tied in different ways around your body, or simply draped over your shoulders to keep off the sun.

Buy it in a blend of natural and synthetic fibers and it will dry quickly and keep you cool. A pure synthetic can be too hot.

A print is better than a solid color because it won't show creases. And believe me, there are wonderful prints around.

Another chic, inexpensive cover-up is a man's T-shirt. You can choose a shrunken tee to show a flash of skin—a look which can be daring and delightful—or consider an oversized tee, which can also look sexy.

If you're wearing a one-piece swimsuit, cover up with a man's shirt. Roll up the sleeves and wear it

Halter tie

buttoned or not. The effect is casual yet sophisticated—perfect for going from the pool to the cabana, or for a stroll along the beach. Buy your shirt in a soft fabric and when you walk against the wind, it'll blow sexily against your body.

You don't want to forget about the cover-ups in the swimsuit department, though. They're so well coordinated and well thought out, you can wear them for a week at a resort. You'll find pants, skirts, dresses, and tops—and these pieces are often a good buy.

Bust tie

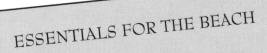

ESSENTIALS FOR THE BEACH

- ✓ Sunscreen
- ✓ Sunglasses
- ✓ Emery board
- ✓ Pareo
- ✓ Large beach bag
- ✓ Big sun hat
- ✓ Plastic bags (to hold wet clothes)
- ✓ Good book or disc player
- ✓ Inexpensive little earrings
- ✓ Flip-flops

Sarong

FOR COLD CLIMATES

If you're going to the mountains or the country for skiing or other outdoor activities, here again, basic neutrals and layering will serve you well.

Start with a great poplin or polyester-filled jacket. It should be a three-quarter length, so that everything you wear—wide pants and slim, long skirts and short—goes with it.

For the greatest versatility, the jacket you choose should be considered not only for country wear but for city wear as well. You can pop it over a sweater and pants and go to the movies in it. (If you're going to use your jacket more for the city, look for a fabric with shine—it's slightly more dressy than wool or wool-blend.)

For the most protection against the elements, look for a style that's water- and wind-resistant, and zips or closes up around your face, backside, and wrists to keep the warmth in. Consider a shearling if you don't mind the weight; it's heavy but it'll keep you toasty.

There are so many fabrics now that keep you warm, but don't let you perspire. It's well worth a trip to a sporting goods store to see what's available for cold weather. With all of these innovative fabrics, you don't have to look bulky. It's just a matter of finding the right fibers and layering them appropriately.

COLD-WEATHER ESSENTIALS

- Thick pair of tights (or thermals)
- Thermal and cotton socks
- Water-resistant shoes or walking boots (anything with a thick tractor sole that grips on icy surfaces; buy them a half-size or one size larger to accommodate thick socks)
- Heavyweight leggings
- Flat knit cotton crew-neck sweater
- Big cozy sweater
- Insulated vest
- Plaid chamois man's shirt
- T-shirts
- Long-sleeved turtleneck bodysuit
- A shawl that wraps comfortably around your shoulders
- Long oblong scarves in extra-fine voiles (for wrapping and looping around your neck)
- Leather gloves—silk-lined
- Quick-drying nylon pants
- Sunglasses
- Cap
- Earmuffs
- Jeans
- Moccasins

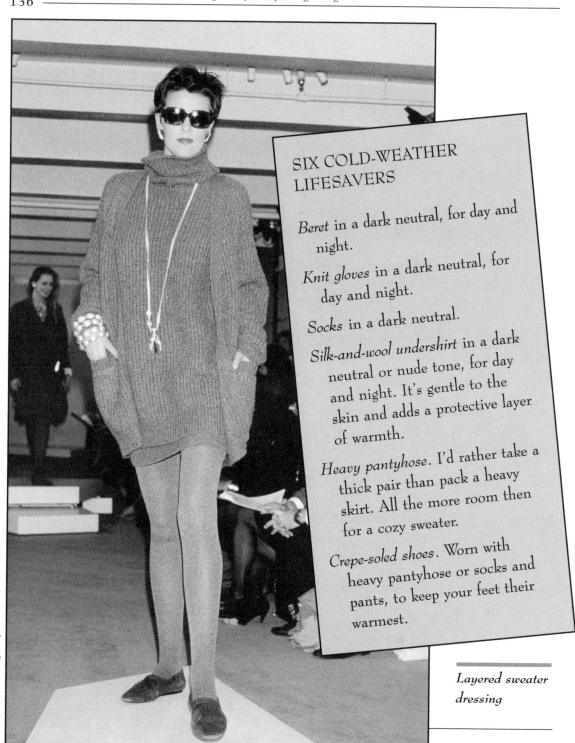

Clothes designed by Donna Karan

SIX COLD-WEATHER LIFESAVERS

Beret in a dark neutral, for day and night.

Knit gloves in a dark neutral, for day and night.

Socks in a dark neutral.

Silk-and-wool undershirt in a dark neutral or nude tone, for day and night. It's gentle to the skin and adds a protective layer of warmth.

Heavy pantyhose. I'd rather take a thick pair than pack a heavy skirt. All the more room then for a cozy sweater.

Crepe-soled shoes. Worn with heavy pantyhose or socks and pants, to keep your feet their warmest.

Layered sweater dressing

Layered separates

Clothes designed by Daniel Hechter

Exercisewear

With all the styles of workout clothes being offered today, there's no excuse *not* to look good when you're exercising. While leotards, leggings, bike shorts, and more have crossover appeal, they're definitely designed with aerobic exercise in mind. Their *first* function: absorbing sweat.

That's where technologically advanced fibers come in. Exercise clothes made of these miracle fibers wick moisture away from your body, ensuring a level of comfort you can count on. If you really are a serious exerciser, opt for the fastest-drying fabrics, such as DuPont's CoolMax™ and Microsupplex™. You won't want anything else.

No matter what your favorite sport or activity, buy the best gear available that's designed for it. If you jog, a sports bra is a must. If you play tennis, your clothes should enhance your movement *and* your game as much as your appearance. And don't overlook your feet. Your choice of footwear is as crucial to your being in shape as your choice of exercisewear.

Get the shoe best suited to your sport. A jogging shoe has no relation to a biking shoe. Look for the proper padding and insulation for your particular type of exercise.

LINGERIE (WITH MORE THAN ONE LIFE)

Feminine lingerie is a mark of a stylish woman, whether she is at work or at leisure. It doesn't have to be silk, but it has to be pretty and sexy. From the moment you start dressing in the morning you should feel good about yourself, and believe me, that good feeling will linger all day. You're lucky, too, because the loungewear and hosiery industries bring out new and exciting styles every season.

The definition of lingerie has changed in today's world and will continue to change. Lingerie isn't just for sleeping anymore. Experiment with body-suits, body shapers, lace-top pantyhose, new panty-hose finishes, lacy soft bras, and sports bras, too.

Of course, beautiful underwear shouldn't show, but you can take pleasure from knowing it's there. I know that when I'm getting dressed in the morning, I feel better putting on pretty lingerie. My viewing audience sees me on television in my designer suits, but I have that secret knowledge of what I'm wearing underneath.

One final word: Buy the best quality you can. Lingerie is not a luxury. It's a way of respecting and treating yourself well.

Clothes designed by Chantelle Thomas

Lingerie

options

ROBES

After a long day at the office, many working women find slipping into a soft, pretty robe can be wonderfully therapeutic. It's nice to go home and not make a decision about what to wear. You really close off the day when you put on a robe.

I have three or four cotton Japanese kimonos, and they're among the most pleasurable things I own. They're all medium-weight fabrics so they

IF YOU CAN AFFORD ONLY ONE GREAT LEISUREWEAR LOOK MAKE IT A . . . *Bodysuit and matching leggings.* Together they form a second skin that can be worn with *any-thing*—from a jacket to a short or long dress. On their own, they're even more versatile. You can even swim in the bodysuit.

work summer or winter. The patterns are pleasing and don't show wrinkles. And the simplicity of a kimono's shape is wonderful—it just wraps around the body.

You really have to find the robe style that works for you and make it a part of your life. It's got to be feminine and pretty—it brings you back to being a woman.

Wrap robe

7

Using Accessories to
Express Your Style

In the last decade, accessories have become almost as important as ready-to-wear clothing. Every specialty store is crowded with different styles of bags, belts, shoes, scarves, and—most important of all—jewelry.

This range of choices and looks makes it as necessary to find your style in accessories as it is in clothing. But it's a fun challenge—and it's

ACCESSORIES THAT GIVE YOU IMPORTANCE

Hat. Even a beret with a pretty pin gives an outfit more panache.
It makes you look more feminine, romantic, even mysterious.
If you've never worn a hat, start experimenting. Hats also have
a practical side: For an important occasion they cover hair
that's not in the best condition, helping you look great.

Sunglasses. They must suit the proportion of your face, and you
must buy them as carefully as you would corrective glasses. Pay
the extra price, and they'll become a signature look. Consider
black, tortoise shell, or bright red. And be sure they actually
keep the sun out—and don't distort your vision.

A classic tote or briefcase. Brown or tan looks good for winter and
summer. It gives you an air of authority everywhere you go.
And apart from holding your work, you can put a lot in it—
even a blow-dryer or large makeup kit.

Wide gold cufflinks worn on the cuffs of a simple black dress or
sweater translate into instant glamour, and dramatize every
motion you make.

Beads. A necklace of three or four rows in different sizes will
bring attention to your face faster than anything else. The
strands should be about choker-length, with beads ranging from
very large to very small. If you have a short neck, look for multiple strands that fall just below your collarbone.

easier to shop because you can wear the outfit you want to accessorize when you go shopping.

One reason for the popularity of accessories is that working women were quick to realize that a few little personal touches could change the look of an outfit, and so double and even triple its use. Another reason is that clothes are becoming simpler as manufacturers find it increasingly expensive to add detailing such as embroidery, trims, and ornamental buttons. Women discovered they must use accessories to put their own stamp on their clothes.

Once designers realized what was happening, they took a serious look at accent pieces—jewelry, belts, bags, shoes, hats, and gloves. Then they broke the old rules and set them aside for good.

What today's designers have come up with are lots of fresh, affordable ideas. Many are also designing complete collections of accessories so their customers can buy individual pieces—a belt, say, or a bag—that don't necessarily match, but have the same mood or feeling. This means each of the pieces can work with others or function separately.

With such a variety of jewelry and accessories to choose from, you have to focus on the style you want. Before you start collecting, you must consider your build, personality, lifestyle, and what suits you best.

JEWELRY

Nothing you wear expresses your personality as much as jewelry. A woman of style coordinates her earrings, necklaces, bracelets, and pins as carefully as the rest of her wardrobe.

Jewelry can be divided into four categories: classic, modern, ethnic, and antique. The boundaries overlap, and you'll probably want to stick to two or perhaps three of the categories. If you wear a bit of everything, the styles will conflict and your look will become diffused.

Again, what's best on you depends on your size, appearance, and personality. If you're short and big-busted, you won't look so great in modern geometric jewelry; conversely, if you're tall and willowy, grandmother's dainty heirloom filigree pin will be lost on you.

Most women can wear bold jewelry, but the proportions are important. If you have doubts, *don't*. If it's not right, all eyes will go to the jewelry instead of your face.

CLASSIC

Some classic jewelry is a must in every woman's wardrobe—strings of pearls and diamond (real or fake) stud earrings are two great standbys. So are slim, round bracelets in metal, wood, or plastic, and strands of sophisticated glass, plastic, or gemstone beads.

These are the most useful pieces for work because they're the most conservative. You'll always feel secure with them, but never daring.

MODERN

Modern jewelry—a choker of large gold beads, a bold orange Lucite pin, large fake-diamond star earrings—makes a strong statement. It should always be the focal point of an outfit. Wear modern jewelry if you have a taste for the dramatic and like to be noticed when you walk into a room.

ETHNIC

Ethnic jewelry is a broad category that can best be defined as looking handmade. It includes stones, beads, woven fibers, metals, and leather—practically anything that can be worked by hand. The looks vary from soft to exotic to high fashion. It rarely looks good in the workplace.

The women who look best in ethnic jewelry seem to be either very sophisticated or earthy.

ANTIQUE

Most women cherish at least one piece of antique jewelry—grandmother's locket or grandfather's watch (if it's a pocket watch you can always wear it around your neck on a ribbon or a chain). But there are also serious collectors who seek marcasite pins, silver bangles, jet beads, and dozens of other heirloom-quality pieces. Sometimes they wear their finds all at once, sometimes one at a time.

The women who wear this style of jewelry usually have a softness or a charm that reflects their interest in the past. If you decide this is your look, read up on antique jewelry. You'll be surprised how valuable it can become over the years.

Precious Jewelry

Every woman should have some precious or semiprecious jewelry that reveals something about her at a glance. If you can't immediately afford what you want, save up for it. Then your hard-earned gift will give you twice the pleasure. Look on your purchase as an investment. The interest generated is just one return you'll see.

The Metals

Throughout the centuries, gold has been the most sought-after metal. It's warm, rich, and glowing. Gold brings light to the face, softens it, and makes it younger looking.

Luckily for us, gold is available in many forms, from the purest castings to gold-plated pieces you can buy practically anywhere. But gold has the disadvantage of coming in many shades, depending on the other metals alloyed with it. At one time, pink gold was considered fashionable; more recently, though, yellow gold has been in style. So when you want to buy earrings to match a particular necklace, take the piece along to make sure the tones are similar.

Silver has two distinct moods. Polished, it's stunning and dramatic, particularly on those with

cool-toned skin. It catches and reflects even more light than gold. A pair of long silver earrings can flash like diamonds. Matte silver has a completely different impact—soft, feminine, and discreet. It has a charm that works with both day and evening clothes.

COLLECTING JEWELRY

The first step is to go through the jewelry you already own. Choose the pieces you love that will create the effect you want. Then photograph them. Studying the photograph will help you decide what your next purchase should be. When you set out to shop for the piece, the photo will help you determine if the design fits in. Each piece should work with almost every other when you first start collecting.

KEEP YOUR EYES OPEN

Magazines are the best source for ideas. Study what the accessories stylists do—in the advertisements as well as on the editorial pages. When you find pictures of models wearing jewelry you like, tear out the pages and take them with you when you go shopping. That way you'll have a good idea of

what you want, and how to wear it for the most modern look.

You need a basic jewelry wardrobe for work. Start your collection with simple accents. They're the ones you'll wear time and time again—studs, hoops, buttons, and drops that are small enough to be worn with a necklace or chains and yet big enough to make a statement and catch the light.

Later on, add studs of pearls or gold-mounted stones—onyx, ruby, and sapphire of the fake variety.

Choose pieces carefully. Not every shape of necklace, pin, or earring goes with every hairstyle, facial shape, or even earlobe. And some color stones will not work as well with your skin tone or your wardrobe.

Remember that one piece of bold jewelry is usually enough for any outfit. If you wear dashing large earrings, for instance, any short necklace or choker will be too much. If you feel you must wear a necklace, go for a long one—to emphasize the style of the earrings.

FIND THE RIGHT LOOK FOR YOU

If there is a particular jewelry shape that suits your style, collect it. If you're under five feet four inches and like pins, collect small ones so you can

wear them together without appearing to be over-powered by them. One very chic petite woman I know collects insect pins that she scatters on the lapel and shoulder of her jackets. The effect is charming.

If you have beautiful wrists and hands, collect bracelets. You can mix and match them to go with different outfits.

If you have a short neck, collect graduated strands of beads that fall an inch or two below the base of your neck to elongate it. For fun, wear two or three together.

Earrings

Earrings are the most important jewelry you'll buy. The right ones bring light to your face and enhance your image. The wrong ones can overpower your look, drag on your ear-lobes and, if too fussy, add years to your appearance.

The best buys are classic shapes—studs, circles, squares, hoops, and drops. Consider three things before you buy: the shape of your face, the size of your ear-lobe, and the length of your neck.

IF YOU CAN AFFORD ONLY ONE PAIR OF EARRINGS, MAKE IT . . . *A medium-size pearl drop set in gold.* You can wear it day and night with your pearls or gold chains.

If your face is round, consider a drop, a square, or a shape that follows the line of your ear. If your lobes are big, avoid small studs, which will make them look even bigger. If your neck is long, look for drops that balance the space between your neck and collar.

Gold is an essential for most women. Its rich gleam adds luxury. Silver is not for everyone, but when it's polished it brings more light to the face, a nice touch for brunettes.

Collect earrings, but stay with substances that will never go out of style—pearls, semiprecious stones, colored glass, bone, or wood.

For a formal evening, rhinestones are a must in either studs or drops. If you can afford it, consider synthetic diamonds. Many today have the glitter of the real thing.

Earrings and necklaces no longer have to match. If you keep your basic pieces simply shaped you will be able to interchange and enrich looks with great enjoyment. You can collect hearts in different styles, metals, and stones and wear them together for a unique look.

NECKLACES

The best necklaces are chains of varying sizes (from fine to large), pearls (fake or real), semi-

precious stones (like coral, turquoise, or onyx), and any of the many types of glass beads.

Lengths are strictly a matter of proportion. If you have a long neck, you can wear thicker beads or stones piled high at the throat. If your neck is thick-ish, you'll do better with graduated stones worn at a longer length.

Remember, jewelry is similar to ready-to-wear clothing. You can layer it, adding more for special effects. Try experimenting; often the most unusual combinations look the best. A heraldic pendant with big fake colorful stones, hanging from a sleek leather whipcord, gives a spirited look to sophisticated strands of pearls.

BRACELETS

A basic wardrobe should include gold and silver bracelets along with wooden and ivory-colored plastic bangles. You can collect bracelets in the accent colors of your wardrobe.

Cuffs are another good investment. Gold-toned cuffs can dress up a sweater faster than anything else. For the office, wear just one. It's a better choice than multiple bangles (which can prove noisy) and makes more of a style statement.

Wear jewelry that's pleasurable to touch.

DOs & DON'Ts FOR JEWELRY

DO as royalty does at Buckingham Palace: Photograph all your jewelry for quick and easy reference. Because the pieces are small it seems so easy to forget what you own. (It's smart, too, if you need to file an insurance claim.)

DO keep jewelry simple for the office; jangly, clanging pieces are distracting in a work situation.

DO try mixing classic jewelry with antique pieces; it's an eclectic look that can be very successful. Also consider pairing gold with silver. If it's done with wit and cleverness, the effect can be marvelous.

DO store your jewelry so you can find what you want quickly. See-through plastic boxes (with a layer of cotton on the bottom) or wicker trays are often easier to use than a jewelry box.

DO hang necklaces and chains on pretty hooks—they'll be easy to spot. At the same time they'll add a special charm to your decor and remind you of your colors.

DO keep silver jewelry in specially treated pouches to prevent tarnishing.

DO experiment and have fun.

DON'T buy jewelry after merely checking the look in a tiny handheld mirror. You need a full-length mirror to gauge if the proportion is right for your body.

DON'T wait until you're rushing out the door to accessorize a new outfit. Remember that proportion is just as important with jewelry as with everything else you wear.

DON'T overlook the size of your features: They'll clue you in to the size of jewelry you can wear. Big lobes need big earrings and small lobes need small earrings.

DON'T buy something "just because it's pretty". Make sure it suits your style and needs.

DON'T buy only costume jewelry. Instead of stocking up on insignificant trinkets, save up and invest in a few real pieces—a gold chain, silver earrings, a string of turquoise beads.

WATCHES

A wardrobe of three types is practical, and they needn't be expensive.

Spend the most money on the all-around watch that you wear every day. An original Rolex Oyster or a Cartier Santos is nice to have, but if you can't afford it, you have a wide choice of less costly classic-looking watches. You can either go for a leather or lizard-strapped tank watch or for something with a stainless or gold-toned band.

A sports watch can be amusingly large and inexpensive, but it must be practical. It should be durable and waterproof at the very least.

If you go out a lot at night, you'll need an evening watch. Try one with a small but easy-to-read dial and a simple black or pretty metal strap. An antique evening watch that still functions will give you a special feeling and look. Your mother might have a "retired" watch that would fit the bill. Or keep your eye out for one at antique shows.

Classic watch

HANDBAGS

While handbags are subject to the same trends as ready-to-wear fashion, certain classic shapes—Louis Vuitton's totes, the quilted Chanel bags with their no-slip gold chains, the envelope clutch—never go out of style.

Your everyday bag should be, for all practical purposes, an over-the-shoulder style of the best quality you can afford. Good leather, when well taken care of, grows more beautiful with age. And quality craftsmanship will endure daily wear and tear far longer than less well made bags. One point to remember is that leather with a small grain or embossed pattern will hide most scuff marks . Your bag should give you pleasure since you use it every day, and it should show you to an advantage. It should last—and be in style—for more than one season.

Be wary of the too big and the very small bag. One of my pet peeves is women who load themselves up like pack mules with huge satchels and totes. They appear dragged down, inefficient. Yet the too small bag looks just as outlandish when it's stuffed fuller and fuller as the day goes by.

A bag should mold to and move with the body. That's the reason Chanel's works so well. The curved shape, the swing from the long chain strap,

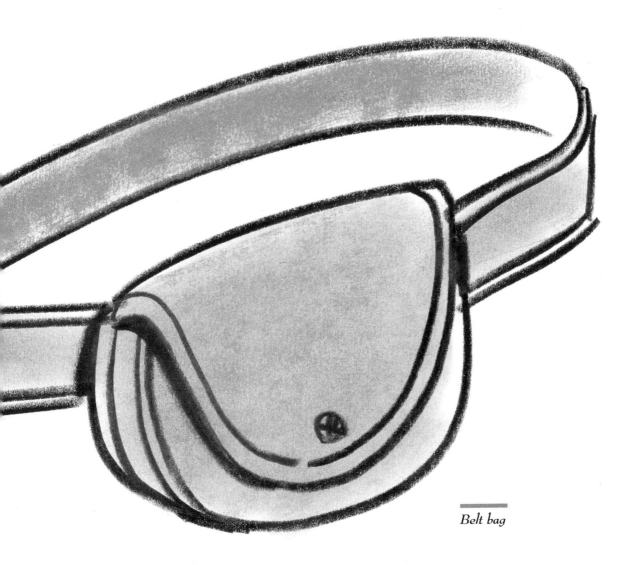

Belt bag

THESE BAGS ARE
ALL YOU NEED

✓ Tote or knapsack

✓ Work bag

✓ Medium-size handbag

✓ Evening bag

the softness of the quilting—all create a feminine yet practical look.

Consider, too, the belt bag. It's appearing at many designer shows, and on the waists of more and more savvy women. It must never be too big—just large enough to carry essentials. When you go shopping, it holds keys, money, credit cards, driver's license, lip gloss, and tissues.

For looks and versatility, one of the best bags you can ever own is a matte-finish, deep-brown fake alligator in a top-quality leather. The stamped pattern hides scratches and scuffs; the deep brown goes with *every* color, summer *and* winter. And the "alligator" finish spells style.

Bags in deep neutral colors—chestnut, burgundy, peanut, even charcoal grey—are always good buys. They work with and give life to the other neutrals in your wardrobe, and they look rich. The contrast of color and texture is endlessly intriguing.

WORK BAGS

If you carry work home, or from appointment to appointment, you'll need a good-quality tote big

Tote bag

enough to hold your files, notebook, and agenda. A tote is the modern answer to the briefcase, and the right one looks just as polished and professional yet far less stiff.

Women executives tell me that a tote can be a girl's best friend when she needs service at airports and hotels. A rich-looking style lends her an authoritative image and a sense of command that others quickly respect.

Another option to consider is the backpack. As designers have realized its importance in the career world and have rendered it in sleek leathers and sophisticated shapes, it's become as stylish as it is practical. A classic look, it carries immeasurable clout both in the office and out.

Whatever your decision, it's best to buy a neutral shade such as brown or tan (light or dark) so you can use it year-round. Black is a smart choice, too, especially if you wear a lot of the color, like I do.

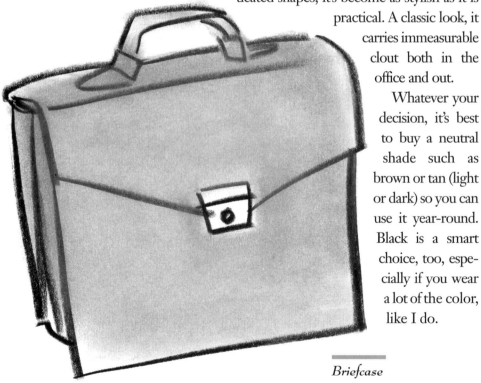

Briefcase

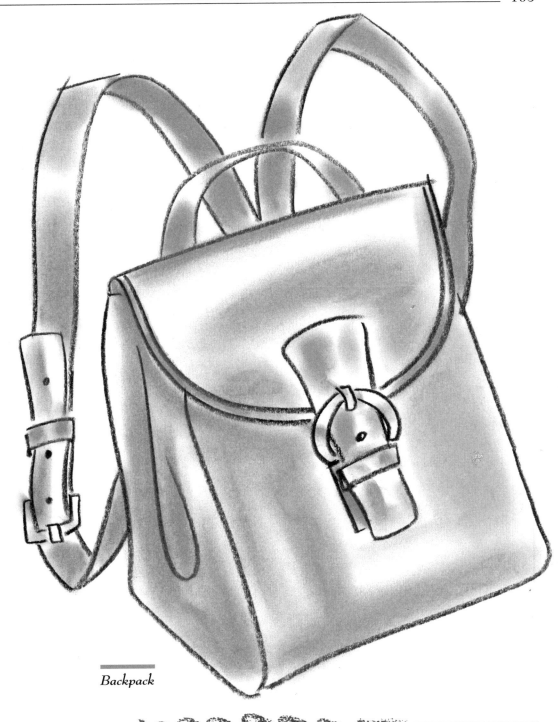

Backpack

Over-the-shoulder bag

To carry your wallet and makeup, choose a small over-the-shoulder bag. It should be big enough so it doesn't look ditzy, but compact enough to go out to dinner. It should be similar in tone to your tote, but never match. (With a backpack you don't need another bag; it easily holds your papers and essentials.)

Again, avoid shine and any other finish that is eye-catching or overly feminine.

The type of material you choose depends upon the season. For warm weather consider canvas, leather, or a combination of both in tan, taupe, or deep beige. For cold weather it should be the best leather you can afford. Choose a dark neutral.

Details on a work bag

DOs & DON'Ts FOR BAGS

DO have at least two work bags in your wardrobe: one for summer and one for winter, each in a basic shade. A leather bag can go all year-round, but you'll find that a new lighter-weight bag will give an immediate lift to all those clothes in your summer wardrobe.

DO make an effort to keep the innards of your handbag simple and clean. Hunting frantically through a bag for makeup or keys gives the impression that you're untidy and disorganized.

DO choose essentials (wallet, cosmetic kit, checkbook) in different styles, but similar deep colors. Should your purse be picked it's just as likely that your cosmetic bag will be snatched as your wallet.

DO check the lining of a bag. It should be toned to match so it looks classy, not cheap. Also pay attention to the construction of the strap. If it's poorly made, it'll cheapen the bag.

DO keep an eye out for inexpensive totes—straw, canvas, or hemp—to use on summer weekends and at resorts. They're functional, and the texture can give both you and your wardrobe a lift.

DO wrap bags in scarves and store them so they're protected from dust. Place handles—especially chains—inside so they don't mark the outside. In fact, it's a good idea to do this every time you return a bag to the shelf or drawer.

DON'T buy a heavy over-the-shoulder bag if you expect to carry it a lot. Fill it and you'll end up with aching shoulders and a cranky expression.

DON'T try to match an evening bag to a particular dress or outfit. A contrasting neutral or metallic looks younger and prettier.

DON'T toss your bag around your car, house, or office like a Frisbee. Take care of leather items to ensure longer life.

DON'T mistake high price for quality. Check out workmanship: well-toned, even stitching; zippers that open and close easily; snaps that stay shut.

DON'T buy a bag that's going to be a problem to close. Buckles and drawstrings can be time-consuming.

should be avoided. Spare and simple looks the most businesslike and orderly, and that says a lot about who you are in relation to your job.

If you travel a lot, invest in an over-the-shoulder bag with a zippered compartment for your passport, traveler's checks, and tickets. Buy it in canvas or leather in a neutral tone, or in a flash of color such as bright red.

EVENING BAGS

If you can afford only one evening bag, make it a no-color metallic. Bronzed grey, just one example, goes with everything. The shine makes any outfit dressier. It adds spark to even neutral-colored evening wear.

While such subtle metallics or neutrals should be your first buy, this is an area in which you can indulge your sense of fantasy and fun. An evening basic could also be an envelope shape, with or

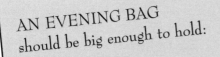

AN EVENING BAG
should be big enough to hold:

✓ Lipstick
✓ Compact
✓ Comb
✓ Money
✓ Tissues
✓ Keys
✓ Business cards

without a shoulder strap, in black silk or satin. You can
then add to your collection other envelopes in brights
(red or emerald green), embroideries (with jewels or
sequins), and richer-hued metallics (gold and silver).

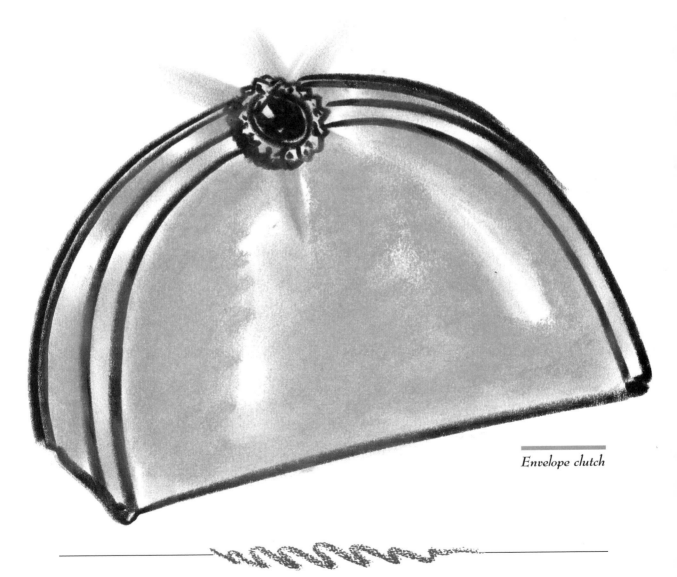

Envelope clutch

Even with shoes, you have to be conscious of keeping to your colors.

SHOES

Here again, put your money into the shoes you wear every day. They should be the best leather you can afford, and you should take care to see that they fit correctly.

DAY SHOES

For daytime, classic pumps are the most useful. For fall and winter, you'll need them in neutrals toned to the clothes you wear. Black, bitter brown, cognac, camel, deep burgundy, or oxblood will go with everything in your wardrobe. Have several pairs in leather or suede (leather is a good all-weather shoe; suede looks more luxurious and dressy), making sure that at least one has a high instep that looks right with pants.

For spring, choose taupe, beige, creamy white, or the crispness of black-and-white spectators. And remember red: A pair of bright-colored pumps can bring to life all your hot-weather dresses. A drop-dead pair of shoes like these is a great splurge, especially if you have small feet and beautiful legs.

In summer, sling-back and open-toe shoes allow heat to escape and help keep your feet from

Medium heel

High heel

swelling. You'll find them immeasurably cooler and more comfortable if you have to walk a lot on the job.

Designers are experimenting with many different fabrics for shoes, from plastic to cotton pique to linen to satin. While these great fashion looks won't last forever—they're not as sturdy as leather or suede—they're basically meant for casual wear.

WORK SHOES

For the professional woman, flats and wedges are just too casual for the office. Boots have a place there as long as they are sleek and simple, and have a low-to-medium heel. A trim leather ankle boot, for instance, is a sophisticated choice with pants.

While a low heel is best with pants, a medium heel (two inches) is smartest with a skirt.

If you're short or average height, go

Ankle boot

Clothes designed by Giorgio Armani

for a medium heel with both pants and skirts; it's more flattering to the leg and gives more presence than a flat.

Avoid high heels most of the time; reserve them for parties. Heels higher than three inches look giddy and unprofessional, and they're hard on your feet. You do want a slightly pointed toe as it elongates the foot and leg, making them look slimmer.

One of the most flattering shoes is Chanel's, with its contrasting toe. It elongates, slims, and adds interest to the foot. And it's delicate, feminine. There's hardly a foot or leg it wouldn't enhance. Many designers offer less expensive versions of this classic pump.

WALKING SHOES

For fall and winter, you'll need walking shoes for city and country. Choose classic oxfords, flat moccasins, or loafers for skirts; ankle boots for pants. Look for a thick crepe or tread sole for the greatest traction in bad weather.

For spring and summer, sandals or open shoes look pretty with long skirts and pants.

Medium-stacked heel

Flat moccasin

Espadrille

Mule

DOs & DON'Ts FOR SHOES

DO stay with a make of shoes (or designer) when you find one that fits well and looks good on your feet. It's a sure way to avoid problems.

DO choose evening shoes with as classic a heel as possible—covered, gently curved, and two to three inches in height. You can wear them with a little bare dress all year-round. And if you don't use them often, then year after year.

DO remember, when buying shoes, to take along whatever you're going to wear with them. You may not be able to try them on together but you'll know if they work.

DO beware of leather in light neutrals. It's difficult to match. Your best bet is to go a couple of shades deeper than the outfit you're trying to match, or choose a two-tone pair.

DO—if you're petite—tone your shoes with your bag. Contrasting colors can cut you in half and make you look even shorter.

DON'T wear a completely flat shoe with any skirt. A little heel height flatters the leg and gives you a more graceful walk. Flats are best with pants.

DON'T wear sneakers to the office. There's a wide choice of good-looking, well-priced walking shoes available today.

DON'T wear matching bright hose with brightly colored shoes. If your legs aren't perfect, it's too much.

DON'T even consider patent leather shoes if your feet are big, or your legs are on the large side. Patent leather makes these features more obvious.

DON'T wear ankle- or T-straps or other fancy shoes unless your ankles are trim and slender.

DON'T get stuck in a time warp. An outdated heel or toe shape can ruin the best look.

You'll need several pairs, of different heel heights, but keep them simple—too fussy a style detracts from your outfits, and too many straps cut into your feet. A simple mule and slip-on espadrille offer relief from tying and buckling, making them two of the easiest shoes in the world to wear. Remember, with a walking shoe especially, comfort is crucial.

EVENING SHOES

Your first choice should be black medium- or high-heeled satin or grosgrain pumps to go with both a dress and evening pants.

Another great look, if your legs are slim, is one with a bow or buckle on the top: It dresses up the shoe and attracts the eye. It looks especially pretty peeking out from evening pants or a long skirt.

Then start collecting:

Low black sandals in silk, grosgrain, satin.

Pretty metallic shoes or sandals—silver, gold, bronze, or a no-color metallic like grey or taupe.

Brightly colored sandals for fall and winter (red or bright green); pale and lovely ones for spring and summer (creamy beige, dusty taupe).

High-heeled satin sling back

HOSIERY

Hosiery is undergoing an enormous change. One can have a wardrobe of pantyhose in a dozen different weights, with or without control-top girdles. There are also myriad colors and patterns. And there are more choices than ever in socks. Anklet, crew, knee, over-the-knee, and thigh-high are just a few of the styles available in a wide range of looks.

The turning point in hosiery came with the introduction of spandex, a stretch fiber with "memory." Since 1962, there's been a tremendous growth in the strengths and colors of yarns such as spandex. The new microfibers are softer, silkier. Sheers, too, are being shown with patterns that look textured, but are really smooth, so they don't snag. The end result is that for a pair of higher-priced pantyhose, you're getting quality like never before—in the fit and the finishing.

Just beware: If you buy revolutionary new pantyhose, you *have* to watch for the size. The industry is still experimenting.

Tinted hose

Hosiery Tips

• Dusty colors are more flattering than clear on most legs.

• Pale taupe pantyhose cast just a shadow on the leg, slimming it beautifully. Yellowish/beige or natural pantyhose widen the leg, flag attention to it.

• Brightly colored hose have no place in the office, but look great for a fun evening out. (If you're in the mood for a dash of color, the cheapest and best place to put it is on your legs. If you can't wear lime green near your face, you can safely wear it on your legs.) Best for day: a neutral such as black, brown, or grey.

• Experiment with color. What looks great on one person may look terrible on you. Brown doesn't look good on all skin types, especially if you're a woman of color. Also, navy may vary from one manufacturer to another, so hold it up to the light for the truest reading.

• Keep in mind that pale cream hues and delicate patterns are not for everyday wear. Choose pantyhose that fit the occasion.

• Play with patterns and make hosiery an accessory you have fun with. Wear leggings and patterned or textured socks.

SCARVES

A scarf was most likely the first piece of cloth a woman wore after she took up weaving. But I doubt she found more uses for it than we have today. Scarves are pretty, versatile, and practical. A scarf can shield you from the sun in summer and protect you from the cold in winter.

Play with your scarves in the privacy of your bedroom so you learn to wear them unselfconsciously. You'll find them among your best friends in your wardrobe. The scarf that's most flattering for you is the one that works with your build and projects your personality.

Squares come in sizes from handkerchief to 54 inches and up. The fabrics range from fine chiffon to loosely woven mohair. The best scarves are soft so they tie and drape beautifully and feel good against your skin. Natural fibers—cotton, silk, and wool—are good, but so are many of the blends. Check to see that the color and the print are almost, if not exactly, the same on both sides so it will look great however you tie it.

A square scarf is your smartest buy because you can do so many things with it. It should always be folded diagonally so the fabric is on the bias. This makes it easier to drape and tie. If you want your scarf to be less bulky, twist it just enough to control

the fullness. The fabric shouldn't look tortured.

The most popular scarf is the 12-by-48-inch. It fills in the necklines of shirts, sweaters, and coats. You can tie it, wrap it around your neck, or let it hang loose. It adds glamour when it has a shine, particularly worn tone-on-tone with an outfit. It works equally well as a sash, or, if you practice enough, as a turban. It can also be tied to the strap of a shoulder bag for dash.

The smallest 12-to-15-inch square can be worn around your head or neck, or tucked into a pocket as it was originally meant to be. Tied around your neck, it's a good sun protector when you're wearing a T-shirt or tank top. Twisted and tied around your forehead, it keeps the perspiration and glare out of your eyes during a hard game of tennis.

Folded diagonally, the 24-to-30-inch square can be worn on the head,

Man's tie

Shawl

DOs & DON'Ts FOR SCARVES

DO practice tying your scarf with a favorite pin. It holds the scarf in place and adds extra flair.

DO make a print scarf with metallic threads a part of your accessory wardrobe. It works easily from day to night, and the subtle glimmer is as pretty as a piece of jewelry.

DO invest in a big, 45-inch-square shawl, in a boldly patterned, lightweight wool—if you're medium to tall in height. It goes over everything, from a suit to an evening dress to a winter coat.

DON'T wear a scarf on your head or around your neck that has a too-busy pattern—it detracts from your face. (A rule of thumb: Save any scarf with distracting prints or multiple bright colors for use as a sash.)

DON'T hesitate to wear clean, simple dots, checks, or plaids—they bring an energy to your face and your look.

DON'T overlook a huge cotton scarf as a summer beach essential. In a gauzy fabric, it's a cool way to protect yourself from the sun.

over the shoulders, or around the waist with the point falling over the hip.

The 36-to-45-inch square is the most useful, and so functional it can become a sarong-type dress in summer. In printed soft cotton, it goes over swimsuits, can be tied diagonally over the bust to make a strapless top, or tied over the hips to make a skirt.

In winter, a 36-by-45-inch scarf adds a dash of warmth and color to anything it layers. Buy a printed one in your colors and you'll find you can wear it day and night. It looks just as smart over a coat as it does over an evening sweater. Take it when you travel and use it as a blanket, or even roll it to make a pillow, and all the while the cheery colors—*your* colors—will make you feel good.

Head wrap

HOW TO TIE . . .

- *A man's tie*: Hang an oblong scarf around your neck with one end lower than the other. Tie a loose knot in the lower end. Place the other end into and through the knot and tighten slightly.

- *A shawl* : Fold a large square into a triangle. Drape over shoulders, or simply knot in front.

- *A head wrap*: Fold a square into a triangle. Bring the widest length down across forehead and side pieces to the back; tie a knot in back to secure.

- *An ascot*: Fold a square into an oblong shape. Hang around neck and loop one end over the other.

Ascot

The largest and most dramatic oblong is the 24-by-92-inch. In wool or cashmere, it's the warmest to own and looks as great filling the neck of a coat as it does over the shoulders of an evening dress.

Oblongs also make the best sashes, tied simply at the waist, gathered and caught with a pin, or twisted tightly and knotted.

> WHEN CHOOSING A SCARF, look for the softness that lends itself to easy tying and draping.

BELTS

The belts to collect first are the textured classics in printed leather—lizard or crocodile, farmed or fake. They add interest to the waist without detracting from the outfit. Buckles should be small and simple—either self-covered, gold, or silver.

The width should range from one to one and a half inches so the belt can go through the loops of a skirt or pant waistband, or cinch the waist of a dress, shirt, or blouse.

Your figure should determine whether or not you match your belt to your skirts or pants. Generally, deep neutral-colored belts are best, because

Chain belt

Clothes designed by Donna Karan

DOs & DON'Ts for Belts

DO buy a simple rope belt as a summer standby. It will go with all your outfits: pants, skirts, and dresses.

DO buy an ornate belt that cinches you at the waist if you're tall and like to wear long skirts or dresses. It can make the simplest look a knockout.

DO invest in a gold chain belt. It's dressy enough for evening and not too dressy for day.

DON'T wear a belt too tightly if you're short-waisted. To create the illusion of a slimmer, longer middle, slightly loosen the belt so it sits on your hips and extends the line of your waist.

DON'T wear too wide a belt; it will detract from your waist.

DON'T neglect the care of your belts. You can have them restitched, cleaned, and freshened up by a leather expert.

they tend to make the waist look smaller. But don't be afraid to mix neutrals. A burgundy belt adds a touch of luxurious color to a grey outfit, and a brown belt enriches navy. For a pulled-together look, tone your belt to your shoes. If you're blessed with a tiny waist and slim hips, don't forget the punch of color either: A bright red belt worn with matching bracelets gives the simplest solid dress great pizazz.

When the hot weather arrives, make the switch from leather to the natural, neutral tones of rope, linen, or hemp. They go with other neutrals as well as brights, pastels, and prints. And their weaves add one more element of interest to an outfit.

Once you have the basics, then go on to discover the fluidity of a chain belt. Wear it loosely cinched at the waist or low-slung on the hips, depending upon your figure. A chain belt is more than functional: It can act as a pretty piece of jewelry, so avoid overdoing it with other accessories.

If you're tall or thin you can wear wide belts, wraps, ties, and sashes to emphasize your waist. Be innovative: Wear large ornate buckles, add a pin to hold a sash in place, tuck in a flower, and use colors that strongly contrast with your outfit.

Hats

Apart from their functional use for warmth in the winter and shade in the summer, hats add drama, mystery, and stature. They give you a presence. Wear a hat and you'll find a difference in the way people treat you.

Start buying your hats with practicality in mind. You'll need a beret for warmth, a rain hat for bad weather. Then add any other styles for fun: a turban, a band that knots in back, or a felt fedora.

Experiment before you settle on your hat. Again, look for proportions. The size of the brim (as well as the hat) must suit the shape of your face and neck. Play around with it. Some women feel better with the brim off the face and some like it down. It's worth experimenting.

To ensure you'll wear your hat again and again, buy it in a color that suits you and your outfits. Most women opt for black, bitter brown, or burgundy in winter, and natural straw in summer.

It takes courage to wear a hat. But when you find one that suits your lifestyle as well as it suits your face, you'll feel like a million dollars.

Beret

Clothes designed by Ralph Lauren

Wide-brimmed hat

Clothes designed by Christian Dior

GLOVES

To most of us, gloves are the most functional of all accessories. But don't pass them by too readily. Gloves can lend a dash of color to spice up an outfit instantly.

Buy them in leather, suede, knitted wool, or cashmere to go with the basic colors of your wardrobe—black, brown, navy, and burgundy. (If you live in a really cold climate, you should buy them lined in silk or cashmere for extra warmth.) For those days when you want to add zing to an outfit, put on a pair of red gloves.

*   *   *

Now that you have a solid accessory wardrobe to build on, allow yourself time to experiment and play. The more you do, the more effectively your style will be expressed.

FOR EXTRA FASHION PUNCH:

- Buy long knit gloves in the same color as your sweater. They'll look luxurious as well as keep you warm.
- Buy leather gloves in a brilliant color—one that sends shock waves against your classic neutrals. If you can, brave yellow, purple, shocking pink, or scarlet. These colors will cheer you on the coldest day.

8

How to Make the Most of Your Looks

Beauty needn't be a big deal. It's all a matter of routine—the simplest routine: having a schedule for keeping your skin and hair clean and nourished, making sure your nails are manicured, and keeping your body in shape. Beauty is also a matter of believing in yourself, of knowing that the way you look counts—not just to your friends and colleagues but, most importantly, to yourself.

Knowing that you look good makes everything easier. Begin the day with a smile in the mirror and you set off on a high note. It seems that once those smile muscles get into place they set off a chain reaction. Smiling makes you feel happier, and the next smiles come faster and more easily. A generous smile can help you manage in the most difficult situations.

Putting on a good face—actually, your best face—is what this chapter is all about.

Proportions Again!

To find your most flattering makeup, study the shape and proportion of your face and features as carefully as you did your figure. You'll find that you fit into one of four basic facial types: oval, round, long, or square.

An oval shape has long been considered the most beautiful—a perfect proportion. Since few of us have perfectly oval faces, we must make do with what we have.

This means playing up your pluses and playing down what you don't like—whether it's a high forehead that needs to be camouflaged or a square jawline that needs to be softened.

But remember that some of the great beauties of

HOW TO DETERMINE THE SHAPE OF YOUR FACE

Round—fuller than other shapes; no definition; no hint of cheekbone.

Long—usually narrow with a long jaw.

Square—a full jawline (more horizontal than diagonal); broad or high forehead; equal width at temples and jaw.

Oval—well-balanced top to bottom; clearly defined cheekbones; diagonal jawline.

TIPS TO MAKE A ROUND FACE LOOK LONGER, SLIMMER

- Keep the concentration of eyeshadow between the inner corner and the center of your eye. Blend out and up toward the outer edges of your forehead.

- Brush on blush in a diagonal line, from under your cheekbone up to the tip of your ear.

- Wear hair softly feathered at sides and brushed forward onto cheeks.

Tips to Make a Long Face Look Shorter, Wider

- Brush on eyeshadow straight across the lid toward temples.

- Sweep on blush straight across from the middle of your cheekbone (even with the pupil of your eye) directly outward to the top of your ear.

- Subtly extend the arch of your brows.

- Wear bangs falling straight down or brush them softly to one side.

- Keep lip color to a medium shade; too dark or bright brings the eye down, down, down.

Tips to Make a Square Face Look Rounder, Softer

- Brush on a triangle of eyeshadow from middle of eye to far outer corner; blend toward forehead corners.

- Apply blush in a soft arc, from middle of cheekbone around and up into hairline.

- Keep brows naturally arched.

- Wear hair full, in a chin-length bob and curled under.

- Emphasize lips with color, as this will bring attention to the center of your face.

Oval

Long

Round

Square

our time have faces that are far from perfect. It's often one outstanding feature that makes a face memorably pretty or striking.

No formula for making up is right for all women. You have to decide what makes you look and feel prettiest and then develop the application routine until you can do it in the shortest amount of time.

Once you've determined the shape of your face, take a separate look at your eyes, nose, and mouth. The makeup you use must play up your best assets and play down your flaws. If you have big features, for instance, you can't wear a lot of color, though you can get away with soft shades.

Learning to compensate for "challenging" features comes with understanding and practice. You might never look as great as the model on a magazine cover but you can look enormously attractive. Experiment until you've achieved the right balance. Once you have the "formula" down pat, it'll work unfailingly for you.

EYES

To make the most of your eyes, start with your brows. The topmost "frame" for your features, brows define your face more than anything else.

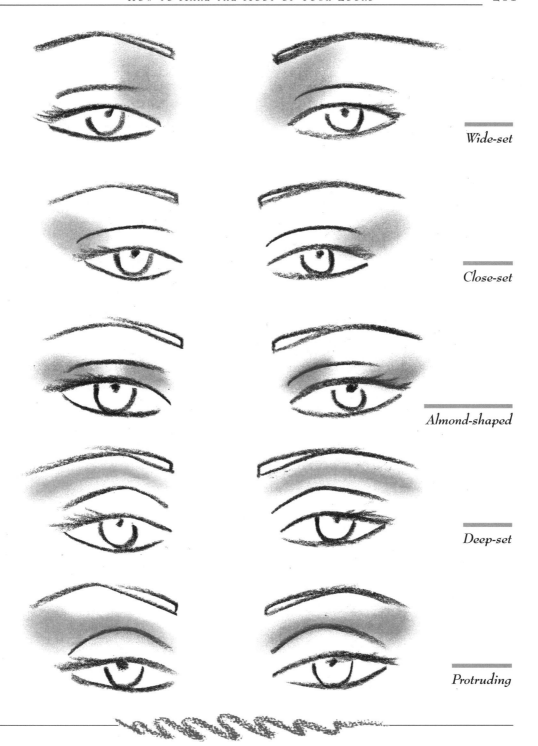

Wide-set

Close-set

Almond-shaped

Deep-set

Protruding

The best look is natural, yet well groomed. By that I mean tweezed and brushed into shape every single day. It takes less than a minute, and the balancing effect this has upon your other features is worth the effort.

Have your brows done by a professional once and it'll be that much easier to maintain the shape—just use it as your guideline and pluck the strays. It's helpful to have a close-up photo taken after the treatment. Then you can study it and see why the shape looks good on you. Put it on your dressing table as a reminder.

Brows should follow the natural curve of the eyes, starting from the line of the nose to slightly beyond the outer corners of the eyes. How thick or thin brows should be depends on whether your features are delicate or strong. Brows should never be so full they appear overgrown, or so pencil-thin they look dated. But thinner brows do look better as you get older.

If your brows are sparse, fill them in with two shades of pencil or powdered eyeshadow—toned to your hair color for the softest, most natural effect. Brush your brows down, out of the way, and then stroke on color in the correct line using both shades. Brush brows back in place and they'll look entirely natural.

Now that your brows are in order, take a close

look at your eyes. Eyes fall under six basic descriptions: round, wide apart, close-set, almond-shaped, deep-set, and protruding. The preceding illustrations will help you target your shape and enhance it with the proper contouring techniques.

NOSE

It may seem that noses come in many categories, but makeup artists generally agree on five: short, crooked, flat, snub, or long.

The good news is you don't need a nose job to resculpt what you have. Some dark and light foundation or contouring powder can rid your nose of bumps or excess length, or compensate for a nose that's snub or too short.

The secret of successful contouring is in the blending. Smudge out the line of contrast between light and dark colors with a makeup brush, sponge, or cotton ball and then dust over with sheer translucent powder.

LIPS

Lips are our most uniform feature, but they also can be too large, too thin, or crooked. Because your

Short   Crooked   Flat   Snub   Long

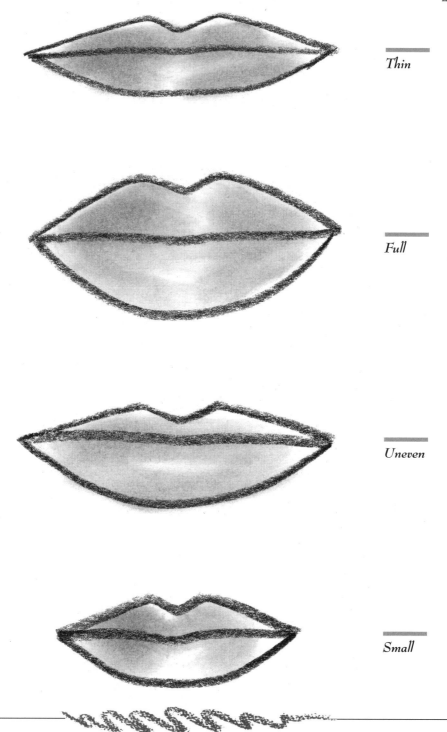

Thin

Full

Uneven

Small

mouth "anchors" your eyes and gives them importance, it needs to be almost as strong a feature.

A lip pencil is your best friend when it comes to plumping, slimming, or evening out your lips. A subtle outline filled in with a matching color (or one half a shade lighter) offers the prettiest and most natural definition.

YOUR BEST MAKEUP

Your most flattering makeup is the one that suits your personal style. Using an expert is the best way to find and develop that makeup.

If you live in or near a large city, look up a professional makeup stylist. There are quite a number of them working with advertising agencies and magazines. Tell the stylist you want a customized makeup look for both day and evening, based on the colors you wear. You'll pay for this service, but once you know the colors that suit you and how to apply them, you'll never again make a bad purchase at the beauty counter.

The cosmetic counter of a department store is another sensible place to start. When you visit for a makeup/color consultation, remember that you're under no obligation to buy everything the salesperson suggests. Take the information they offer (free

MAKEUP TIPS

- Put on a sunblock when you go outdoors—on face, hands, and arms (where skin ages fastest).

- Use an electric or regular manual sharpener to fine-point your makeup pencils. The sharper (note: as opposed to rounded) the point, the easier to work with and the more precise the line.

- Carry a makeup kit that duplicates the one you have at home—so touch-ups always match.

- When applying mascara to bottom lashes, hold a tissue under the eye for a no-smudge finish.

- For an even application of liquid liner, tilt your head back slightly, hold your eye half-open, then smooth the lid slightly, gently, and run brush as close as possible to lashline.

- Follow blush with a sweep of translucent powder for a no-seam finish.

- If you favor an eyebrow pencil, stroke it against the bristles of your brow-brush; *then* brush color directly on hairs to fill in for a natural effect.

- Sweep translucent powder *under* eye before applying shadow to lid; then easily brush off fallen color particles.

of charge!) and use it intelligently. Ask for a chart on how to apply the makeup, and take along your trusty camera (ask the stylist to take a few shots).

Several cosmetic companies, including Prescriptives, Princess Marcella Borghese, and Origins, divide their makeup into four color groupings. Each color grouping includes everything from foundation to lip color so all products are color-toned. The companies provide a chart on each product that shows you how to best apply it.

Beauty essentials

TIPS FOR MAKEUP THAT LASTS ALL DAY

• Use a liquid liner or line eyes with a powdered shadow. Apply shadow with a wet, tapered brush to ensure no-fade, no-smudge definition. (Eye pencil contains wax, which melts as the day wears on.)

• If you only use pencil, layer it with toned shadow for staying power—and a smoky effect.

• Brush on one of the new lash bases to which mascara can cling. Or, dust lashes with translucent powder before you stroke on color.

• Apply light foundation to lips (make sure they're dry), then use lip pencil to outline and fill in mouth. Powder over and layer with lipstick for color that won't quit or feather.

• Apply pressed (rather than loose) powder for nonstop, nonstreak coverage.

• Set makeup (after touch-ups, too) with a fine mist of water.

• Smooth concealer on lids as well as beneath eyes; shadow will cling to lids and stay true longer.

Clothes designed by Yves St. Laurent

However you arrive at your makeup system, the fun begins when you bring your purchases home. I really enjoy making up. Smoothing cool, creamy foundation over my face, sweeping on silky powder—these are sensual experiences that give me a great deal of pleasure. This ritual lifts my mood in the morning before I set off to work, and it's a pick-me-up in the evening when I'm getting ready for a party.

GREAT BEAUTY-GEAR INVESTMENTS

Folding mirror: it magnifies to show if makeup really is correct.

Manicure: once a week, every other week, or at least once a month; pedicure: once a month. The most beautiful nail shapes are oval (to elongate) and a softened square.

Styling brush: an all-in-one blow-dryer with brush attachment (or hot-air brush, straightener) cuts down on styling time.

Spray mister: to rehydrate skin, set makeup.

Heavy, all-purpose cream: for softening lips, cuticles, hands, heels.

Classic brush collection: face brush, cheek color brush, two eyeshadow brushes, comb-and-bristle eyebrow/lash brush, and lip brush.

Good pair of tweezers.

Good beauty tools are an essential part of making up—for the pampering aspect as well as the finished effect. A gentle sponge and big soft brush feel wonderful when I put on my foundation and blush, and they yield a much smoother line than my fingers do.

I do my own makeup confidently because I know the rules of my face. It's long and very European-looking; all concentration is in the middle. I need horizontal lines—liner and shadow extended slightly beyond my eyes, blush brushed straight across my cheekbones—to break up that length and make my face look shorter.

The top makeup experts I work with say a matte face is the prettiest, most professional, most natural-looking face. Neutral-toned, flat-finish shadows and powders strengthen your features without overwhelming them (plus they won't show wrinkles—reason enough to love them!). And the color stays put for hours. When your working day extends into evening, add more color for drama and a touch of gloss for life and sparkle.

A totally natural face—no makeup at all—is not stylish. Every woman needs a little color, a little gloss, to give her vitality. Of course you have to be realistic about your lifestyle, your skin tone, the size of your features, and your age. Just a touch of vibrancy can make you feel so much better, especially on days when you're tired and stressed-out.

My three rules for your best look, head to toe, are…
- *Know yourself (that includes your colors and proportions).*
- *Follow the rules and routine that make you look great.*
- *Enjoy doing it. Make it fun! Then you'll have style.*

YOUR BEST HAIRSTYLE

For the working woman, the best length of hair is medium—a cut that falls between the ears and the shoulders. Only beautiful young girls can successfully manage very short hair. I've found that even models with perfect complexions and features let their hair grow out again after a season or two of having it short.

Clothes designed by Michael Kors

Soft, touchable hair

Hair makes a woman feel feminine, so you'll be happier if you have some length to play with. Free-flowing, below-the-shoulder hair is for the very young. It's charming on children and teenagers, but it looks untamed and unprofessional on women at work. If you want to keep your hair long, tie it back neatly off your face. Or use any of the classic hair accessories—from sleek headbands to big pull-back clips or pretty bows.

Clothes designed by Isaac Mizrahi

Medium-length curly hair

DOs for Healthy Hair

DO remember the most attractive hair is soft, shiny, with a color that looks natural, whether it is or isn't.

DO go to a reliable hair salon if you decide to color your hair. Watch the procedure carefully, ask questions, and even make notes. Armed with information you'll do a much better job if you color it yourself.

DO go back to a professional every fourth or fifth color renewal. Believe me, it's worth the cost.

DO photograph a new hairstyle. Whether you love or loathe the cut, the photo is a useful record. Study it to see how the proportions work with your features, neck, and body. Take it with you as a reminder for your next cut.

DO condition ends only as needed, so roots don't get oily and flatten your look.

DO try to rinse for a full two minutes after conditioning to remove all residue (which can weigh hair down).

DO rinse hair, once or twice a week, with a water-and-vinegar or water-and-lemon juice solution to add shine, cut residue. Use a tablespoon of vinegar (or lemon juice) to a cup of water.

DO avoid excessive use of styling lotions. They dry and flatten hair.

DOs for a Good Haircut

DO consider a blunt cut, especially if you've got fine hair. It will look fuller and be easier to manage. If you're blessed with thick hair you can afford to experiment and consider different styles.

DO leave the stylist alone; don't chatter. After you've told her what you want, relax and watch her work. This allows her to concentrate, while you watch, to make sure she cuts the length you want.

DO get a consultation while you're in street clothes and your hair is dry so the stylist can determine your proportions and best possible style.

DO make sure you're always sitting properly. An upright position ensures a more even, balanced cut.

Hair should also be minimum-care. You should be able to shampoo and blow-dry it in twenty minutes. If the upkeep takes longer, reconsider your style.

The basis of any successful look is the cut. A good one works with, not against, the natural texture of your hair. Ideally, after combing or brushing, your style should practically fall into shape.

To find the right look for you, first decide on a style that suits your facial and figure proportions. A woman with a petite frame should avoid the height-cutting lines of a fluffy style with bangs, while a woman over six feet can't get away with a cropped hairstyle.

Clothes designed by Goeffrey Beene

*Day or evening
Braid*

If you see someone with a great style or cut, don't be shy—ask her where she has her hair done and who does it. A look that catches your attention is the best reference you can get. Or make an appointment with a well-recommended stylist. Ask to see him when you first go into the salon. The stylist will be able to see the texture of your hair when it's dry, and how you look in your clothes. From that quick view, he'll have a better idea of your lifestyle and the effort you usually put into your looks. Discuss your ideas with him, and show him any haircut pictures you might have collected so he has a clear understanding of what you like. Then, you'll stand less chance of being disappointed.

TV directors like me with my hair brushed off my face. They feel it projects more authority on camera. But a bit of bang camouflages my high forehead and balances my long face.

Clothes designed by Ralph Lauren

EVENING STYLES

Having a hairstyle that's neat and tidy for work doesn't mean you can't have a glamorous mane at night and during the weekend.

Blow-dryers, hot rollers, mousses, and gels all can help you change your look quickly and easily. And you have a choice of dozens of ribbons, bows, combs, bands, and barrettes designed to give hair a dramatic lift.

Classic flip

Bob

Clothes designed by Oscar de la Renta

Nails

At an interview or during a presentation, your hands are always in the spotlight. Overlooking their grooming could be your worst mistake.

For great-looking hands, count on a manicure once a week. If nails are fragile or chip easily, plan on a polish change between manicures.

You can save time and money by doing your nails at home. But treat yourself to the services of a salon professional every four to six weeks. She will correct the shape of your nails and treat your hands to a softening massage. Manicures are one of the best, most inexpensive indulgences.

And after all, aren't you worth it?

Five-Step Manicure

- Remove old polish.

- File nails into a rounded or softly squared shape; wash hands.

- Massage cuticles and hands with good moisturizing cream, or soak in soapy lukewarm water, or immerse in heated moisturizing cream for 2–3 minutes.

- Push back cuticles with wet washcloth, and carefully trim if necessary.

- Apply base coat, two coats of polish, and top coat. (Allow each coat to dry in between.)

Hand-Care Tips

- Moisturize hands after every washing.

- Hydrate skin by drinking lots of water. (If traveling, double up on water intake and moisturizer application.)

- Soak hands in warm olive oil for several minutes each week: It softens cuticles as well as hands, plus strengthens your nails.

- Once a month, before going to bed, smooth moisturizer (or a moisturizing face mask) on your hands and cover with white cotton gloves. If hands are really chapped, your body heat will "seal in" needed emollients.

- Treat yourself to a professional manicure at least once a month.

Five-Step Pedicure

- Remove old polish.

- Blunt-cut nails with clipper; file straight across.

- After soaking feet in soapy water, use pumice stone on rough spots and heels. Massage heavily with cream.

- Massage toes with intensive moisturizing cream.

- Apply base coat; follow with two coats of polish.

IF YOU CAN AFFORD ONLY ONE MONTHLY BEAUTY SPLURGE, MAKE IT . . .

A body massage. It makes you aware of your body, and it's the most relaxing, refreshing thing you can do for yourself. You need to look after yourself and to keep up with your regular grooming routines—and the best way to do that is to stay in constant touch with your body.

FOOT-CARE TIPS

- Moisturize morning and night.

- After a bath or shower, smooth away calluses and rough spots with a pumice stone.

- Always fully dry feet and dust soles with powder or cornstarch to reduce chances of fungal infections.

- Get professional treatment for persistent corns and calluses.

- Once a month, before bed, massage feet with emollient-rich cream; cover with white cotton socks overnight for an eight-hour softening treatment (the warmth from the socks will help your skin to better absorb the cream).

Beautiful skin . . . beautiful hair

Epilog

Your Style Does Not Stop Here!

I believe that style is an informed expression of your inner self. And while self is very important, being informed is equally important. To choose something "just because you like it" is not enough. You need to understand the choices you make—how they fit into and enhance your life.

To be informed about the complexities of what gives you pleasure opens you up to new possibilities—and even greater enjoyment and self-satisfaction. It's only when you ask yourself "*Why* do I like that?" that you can consistently make the right choices. Once you gain a sense of *why* you like what you do, your personal style begins to develop.

Each day offers a whole series of choices that help define you as an individual. Some questions are as basic as whether to slick your hair back with a headband or wear it down, or to apply clear or red polish to your nails. Ideally, the decisions you make should be based upon who you are, how you perceive yourself, and how you want others to see you. It's a combination of these little moment-by-moment, day-by-day choices that creates a total image.

To make the wisest decisions, you need to study what's out there. Keep abreast of trends shown in the fashion magazines and adopt the ones that "fit" your personality and body. When you're aware of all the available options (and that means opening yourself to possibilities you might not consider initially), *then* you're making informed selections. That doesn't rule out looking to the past for inspiration—perhaps a book on Chanel, a 1930s movie, or an Impressionist painting. Once inspired, you must develop an awareness of how those resources can be applied to your life in order to complete the cycle and bring these ideas to the present.

For most of us, finding a personal style is not something that's done casually. I've been working at it all my life. And since never-ending change is a fact of life, your style—like mine—will have to undergo similar adaptations to stay strong and current. You have to be aware of the changes in your life—whether occupational, emotional, or physical (as your body matures). It's also important to figure out how each change affects you.

It's a telling statement when you see women with the same overall look they had ten years earlier. For some people, it may be an unconscious way of holding onto their youth. But an inability or refusal to adapt or adjust your style is a sign of resistance to change. Women who *don't* change as the world evolves around them look old-fashioned whether they're 29 or 59. Style can't flourish when you limit your own vision of yourself: Life moves on, and you move on.

The more you know, the more you can appreciate and respond to your style. Over time, your selections will be spontaneous. If someone asks why you chose a certain accessory, the answer is immediate: It connects with something deep inside you. The process of knowing what's right becomes second nature to you.

And that's the end result of style: It gives you pleasure, it helps you express yourself, and makes you feel good about who you are. It gives you a greater sense of self and the fulfillment that comes with expressing yourself in a creative way.

Think of the pleasure you get from seeing someone who's really well-dressed. Without even knowing you, they've brought a touch of beauty into your life for that moment. Style is about giving to others as much as it's about giving to yourself.

Between friends, style can enhance the relationship. Think of all the times your best friend has complimented you on a jacket or pin you've worn. Your selection of clothes and jewelry adds pleasure to her life—just as her choices do to yours—and the respect and love that you have for each other as individuals is reaffirmed.

When you have style, you make the world a prettier place. By reaching inward, exploring and recognizing what makes you happy, you have an opportunity to share some of that view of life and the things you deem beautiful. And that enriches the lives of others.

Wearing things that you consider lovely—things that are tactile, colorful, and pleasing to the eye—heightens your own sense of connection with the world. You get to share its physical resources in an intimate way, and bring them down to the most personal level.

Style extends far beyond the clothes you wear.

Clothes designed by Sonia Rykiel

Style is *ongoing*

It's also the way you choose to furnish your home, entertain, and display the little things you collect.

The things with which you surround yourself are all, in one way or another, a reflection of your style. There should be a certain kind of unity among your possessions—a harmony that's subtle, yet rich in diversity.

As with anything you consider making a part of your life, evaluate how your choices fit into your vision of yourself. The more you question and analyze, the less random—and more right—your choices will be.

Ultimately, style is a quality that grows out of a lifetime of experiences, options, and training. Look inward and you'll find style—*your* own wonderful, unique sense of style. It's never too late to give yourself the pleasure.